T0353750

Illuminating
the Alzheimer's
Path

*Living in the Light While Walking
in the Darkness of Dementia*

DONNA BROWN BENTON

AuthorHouse™
1663 Liberty Drive
Bloomington, IN 47403
www.authorhouse.com
Phone: 833-262-8899

Because of the dynamic nature of the Internet, any web addresses or links contained in this book may have changed since publication and may no longer be valid. The views expressed in this work are solely those of the author and do not necessarily reflect the views of the publisher, and the publisher hereby disclaims any responsibility for them.

Any people depicted in stock imagery provided by Getty Images are models, and such images are being used for illustrative purposes only.
Certain stock imagery © Getty Images.

This book is printed on acid-free paper.

ISBN: 979-8-8230-4121-8 (sc)
ISBN: 979-8-8230-4123-2 (hc)
ISBN: 979-8-8230-4122-5 (e)

Library of Congress Control Number: 2024927682

Print information available on the last page.

Published by AuthorHouse 04/10/2025

authorHOUSE®

To each person who will live with Alzheimer's and to each of us who will journey with them, care for them, and love them.

To researchers and all those dedicating their life's work to the cures for Alzheimer's and all forms of dementia.

A Paradigm Shift

THE WAY I often observed Alzheimer's depicted was as a very dark, negative state to be endured. I saw it portrayed only in black and white and in newspaper headlines, such as "Alzheimer's Has a Heavy Price for All" and "Alzheimer's Devastating Legacy." I believe it's more than alliteration that the word "devastating" is so often used to describe this disease; it's almost as if it's a compound word—"devastating-disease." I recently came across an obituary of someone I know. It read, "The person died of the devastating disease, Alzheimer's." I cringed both at the word "devastating" and because I would never want Alzheimer's to define my husband's life. In dialogue with people whose loved ones had the disease, I only heard the same litany of grievances—"Alzheimer's took my wife away," "My mom doesn't know me anymore," "My dad is a vegetable now," "Help me end my life if I ever get this disease," and so on.

Since I had no previous up-close-and-personal experience with Alzheimer's, I entered this world without my own framework or belief system to bring to Doug's diagnosis. Thus, without realizing it, I initially brought a very fixed mindset based on the conventional, accepted assumptions, beliefs, and descriptions of dementia. I felt depressed and defeated for both Doug and for our family. I was certain we'd never enjoy a happy day again, that I'd have to institutionalize him, that it was—in fact—a devastating disease and he soon wouldn't know us, and on and on. I was stuck in a loop. There had to be another way to live. I knew if we were going to get through this, and if I wanted to support Doug and our daughters through this, I had to achieve a better headspace. I had to let go of how I was expecting our lives would unfold.

In the middle of this dark period, I had to take an out-of-town trip. I was hustling through an airport to make a flight when I happened to look up and see a billboard that stopped me in my tracks. It was a light blue, luminously bright, visual representation of dementia. I couldn't believe what I was seeing—Alzheimer's in conjunction with the three words "compassion, care, community." These words were not usually used in association with this disease. I didn't care if I missed my flight; I had to stop to snap a photo to serve as a permanent reminder to myself that there were people somewhere who viewed Alzheimer's differently. This display panel was in juxtaposition with the black-and-white, depressing way I was used to seeing dementia portrayed. I knew nothing about the sponsoring organizations, but I loved their names: "Cure the Cloud" and "Dementia Friendly America." As I boarded the plane, I sensed something shifting in my thought process about dementia. I was about to take flight both literally and figuratively. If I can dream it, I can do it.

A common mantra I preached while raising our daughters was, "If you can't change your situation, change your attitude." It was now a certitude that our situation, Doug's diagnosis and prognosis, was not going to change. Battling against it and resisting reality was not going to change anything. I needed to accept, heed my own mantra, and change my attitude. If I couldn't change what happened, I could decide how I chose to respond. I could live out of our circumstances or I could live out of a vision.

During this period of crisis, I did much reflecting and realized I already had inside me a lot of truths that I had learned throughout my life. I had gleaned this wisdom from past experiences, lessons learned, grace and growth, and living and loving. I now needed to draw on these insights. Some examples of applications of this wisdom were to recognize that I had adopted a fixed mindset about Alzheimer's. I didn't need to accept this conventional wisdom, accept the limits being prescribed, or settle for the default position. I could slowly transition to a growth mindset about Alzheimer's. That change would allow me to be curious and creative, resulting in approaching Doug's dementia differently. I could have an expansive mindset. I could reimagine dementia. I've often been advised that how you see is what you see. This insight made me want to choose a different lens, a different perspective, to see dementia differently. I started envisioning our remaining life together as more satisfying. I created a vision board, including images of possible cruises to Alaska and Hawaii, a father of the bride walking his eldest daughter down the aisle, and happy couples celebrating their twenty-fifth wedding anniversary. Thoughts can become actions. Also, words matter and have the power to shape and influence the future. Thus, I decided to cease speaking of Alzheimer's as the "devastating-disease" and chose to thoughtfully speak about it more objectively.

Though I was unaware, since it was happening slowly, I was experiencing a paradigm shift from where our Alzheimer's journey began. This shift was the result of constant small, and sometimes imperceptible, choices and attitude adjustments that I was able to make as we moved forward. Eventually, there was a major change in how I thought and acted, a tipping point that upended and replaced my prior Alzheimer's paradigm. This change had a profound and positive impact on my life and Doug's life while we continued living with dementia.

Viktor Frankl, who survived the desolate World War II concentration camps, put it this way: "Everything can be taken from a man but one thing: the last of human freedoms—to choose one's attitude in any given set of circumstances, to choose one's own way."

DONNA BROWN BENTON

Alzheimer's has heavy price for all

Alzheimer's devastating legacy

community

Alzheimer's took my wife away

DONNA BROWN BENTON

ILLUMINATING THE ALZHEIMER'S PATH

happy

50 DAY of BIRTH

early-onset
alzheimer's

I'm too young to have
Alzheimer's disease

Doug's Day of Birth
March 21,
1st Full Day of Spring

Too Soon

DOUG ARRIVED IN this world two weeks after his due date. I can testify that this was the last time he was late for anything, and he made up for lost time ever since. How true to form that he was diagnosed with early-onset Alzheimer's.

Early-onset is often hard to diagnose. For patients presenting at such a young age, healthcare providers routinely don't initially look for a dementia diagnosis. The process can be long and frustrating. That certainly was true in Doug's case. No matter what age one is diagnosed with dementia, I'm certain the person who receives the news and his or her family feel it comes too soon. "Early-onset," or "younger-onset," is defined as any age under sixty-five. Doug was fifty years old at the onset of his symptoms. In the dementia clinics we visited for years, we met some younger-onset patients in their thirties and forties.

The duration of younger-onset is different in every case. We were told that sometimes the disease advances quickly, and in some cases, it's long, perhaps in part because younger patients may have stronger, healthier bodies. Luckily, we drew the long straw. Doug's progression moved more slowly. We got sixteen more years together. I was so grateful to have Doug every day of those sixteen years, as I knew we were living on borrowed time. It was good that I was also young and able-bodied so I could care for Doug physically and meet all the dementia needs.

I'm painfully aware that, like dementia, other life-changing illnesses can occur earlier than they typically do. I can only speak about our experiences with early-onset dementia. We share the fallout from Doug's illness, not to host a pity party but to heighten awareness of early-onset Alzheimer's so we can sensitively respond to those currently dealing with this and for those who will face it in their future.

In order of importance, I first share some of the many ways an early-onset diagnosis affected our family. Our daughters were thirteen and sixteen years of age at the time of their father's diagnosis. In an attempt to be supportive, their friends often said to them, "I understand. My grandfather has Alzheimer's too." But this wasn't our daughters' grandfather. It was their father. It's developmentally appropriate for adolescents to be embarrassed by their parents. Among other things throughout their teen years, our girls were embarrassed by my loud laugh, that I dressed too "matchy-matchy," and that I drove a car that was too old for them to be seen riding in. Though they said little about it, I sensed our daughters were sometimes embarrassed by aspects of their father's affected appearance and behaviors.

Due to our decreased family income and increased associated expenses, both girls had to finance their own college years. Unfortunately, both are still burdened with student loan debt. Of course, the too-early loss of their dad continues. The father of the bride was not physically there to walk our youngest daughter down the aisle. Sadly, Doug was also deceased before our three grandchildren were born to our daughters.

Doug's employment was another major area affected by early-onset. His job was very detail-oriented, and not long after diagnosis, it was clear to both Doug and his employer that he was struggling and no longer able to produce and perform at the level the position required. His mental and emotional health suffered from the sadness of this loss. Doug went from being the primary breadwinner one day to providing no income the next. He struggled with the resulting loss of identity and self-worth.

Early-onset affects financial wellness. There were serious financial and other consequences for us. In addition to the loss of salary, Doug's loss of employment meant losing his company-provided health insurance and the added cost of COBRA. An early stepping down from work also minimizes retirement and stock option benefits as well as personal and company contributions to one's 401(k) and pensions. We were in the middle of paying off a thirty-year mortgage on our home. Doug also had to give up his side hustle of playing in a rock and roll band. As a musician, this was a profound personal loss, and the loss of bonus income was a double blow.

Mom,

Since my diagnosis, I have been giving getting my affairs in order. Regarding your new will...

"Just wanted you to know good wishes because one of my worst fears is that I won't be here to provide for J & E & Donna.

Doug's journal entry reflects his financial fears for his family's future.

DONNA BROWN BENTON

My employment was also affected. After almost two decades of teaching in parochial schools, I had to transition to public schools for an increase in salary, health insurance, and retirement benefits. It was difficult to start over at the bottom of the ladder. Since I needed to continue to work full-time, there was the added cost of adult daycare and then an in-home caregiver during my workday. Due to my work schedule, I was forced to pass on many services and activities that could have benefited Doug and me. I remember in particular an eight-week program offered and paid for by a pharmaceutical company. Lunch and care were provided for the patients, while their caregivers separately ate lunch and learned through an informational and supportive session. When I inquired if it could be offered at dinnertime as well, they responded that Alzheimer's patients and their caregivers are usually elderly and don't venture out in the evening.

Additionally, since Doug was not yet sixty or sixty-five, he did not qualify for many services, such as Social Security, Medicare, Meals on Wheels, a shuttle service to attend a local senior center, and more.

I describe our entire early-onset experience as a time warp. The diagnosis picked us up and propelled us into the future. Our lives accelerated twenty years forward. We were instantly immersed in end-of-life issues. But no one is promised tomorrow. I miss the twenty years we lost to early-onset, but I'm grateful for the thirty-five years of life we had together.

In retrospect, details or issues resolved or receded in importance. What really matters lived on. Through it all, we remained rich in love.

DONNA BROWN BENTON

Unspeakable

I WAS OFTEN PUZZLED by a pattern of sharing that my friends or colleagues sometimes exhibited. There was a noticeable hesitance, followed by a cross-examination to determine if I could keep a secret. Finally, often in a whisper, they shared an upcoming divorce, a recent diagnosis, or some other fraught situation.

As Doug and I were just beginning to digest and process his diagnosis, I recalled my experiences of this slow sharing of news. My past perplexity was replaced with some clarity.

Silence was Doug's and my state of being. There were no words shared: unspeakable even to each other. We were communicating on a nonverbal level, deeper than words could express. Our exchanges took the form of holding hands as we lay awake most of each night, enveloped in each other's arms during the days. I certainly wasn't ready to talk about it all and assumed, by Doug's relentless silence, he wasn't ready either. I was taking my cues from my introverted husband since this was primarily his prognosis. We'd wake up some mornings and wonder if this was a nightmare or something truly happening. We were in the first stage of grief—denial. Our physical sensations of light-headedness and being in a fog were our bodies' defense systems in action. We were in a state of shock, and our minds were protecting us from taking in more reality than we could handle at one time. Gradually, we were able to verbalize with each other what, until this point, had been going on only on the inside of each of us. We slowly gave voice to emotions. It finally was right and supportive to share with each other. Once we had told ourselves our feelings about the diagnosis, and then told each other, we were prepared to tell others, although reluctantly.

Of course, our adolescent daughters had to be the first to be told. Imagining how it would be received by them, how could we bring ourselves to deliver this diagnosis of their dear dad?

Both Doug's mom and my mom and all of our siblings knew of our extensive testing and diagnosis-seeking process. They were anxious for answers. This was not what we had hoped to share, but we needed to bring ourselves to tell them.

The sharing process continued slowly, a few people at a time. Some friends were upset with me over the time that had elapsed from diagnosis to my sharing the news. I offered each of them, as an explanation, my new and insightful learning gleaned from this experience. Put simply, you can't tell others until you can tell yourself. Those who had also experienced an unspeakable time in their lives knew this to be true and agreed. The rest will understand someday after their own unspeakable life events.

Much later, I felt validated about this early stage of silence when celebrities I admired shared their own similar stories. I heard Michael J. Fox, during a television interview, talking about his Parkinson's diagnosis. He said it took him seven years to get his head around it before he shared the news with his fans. Similarly, there was an article in a 2021 issue of *AARP* magazine about Tony Bennett having Alzheimer's disease. The article was titled "Breaking the Silence." The tagline explained, "For four years, Tony Bennett and his family have kept his secret. Now they have decided the truth must be told." Learning of others also slowly sharing their stories, confirmed to me that perhaps it's a universal experience.

So now, when people don't quickly share certain information with me or haven't yet told me what I already know from another source, I wait in silence and with patience and love, not puzzlement. I now understand; they also can't tell others until they can tell themselves.

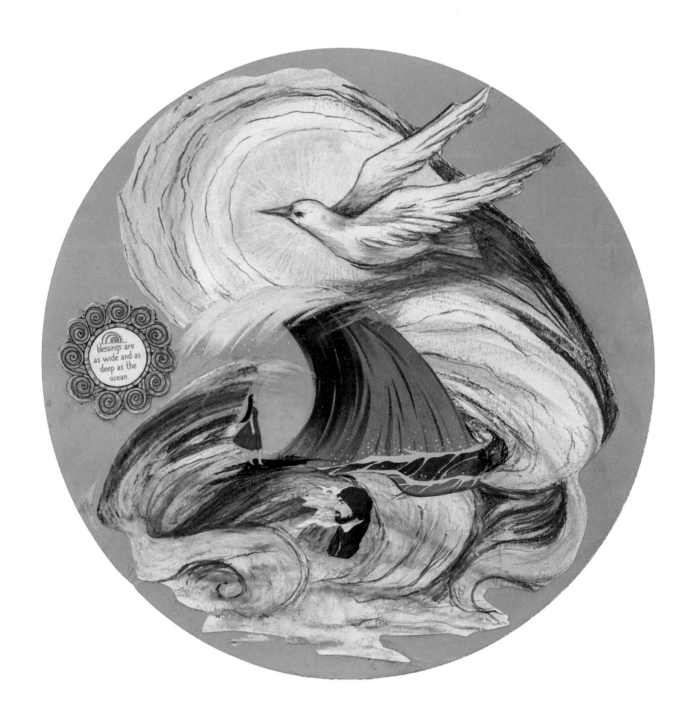

blessings are as wide and as deep as the ocean.

DONNA BROWN BENTON

No Storm Can Shake My Inmost Calm

DOUG AND I were both ocean lovers and goers. Because of this shared attraction, we honeymooned in Boynton Beach, Florida. Our romance with the ocean continued throughout our lives together. Repeatedly, when we needed to relax and renew, we'd retreat with our family to the beach. The ocean always had a soothing and meditative effect on us. The vastness made us realize anew that we were part of something larger than ourselves. The absence of schedule and technology, plus the magnificence of water and sunlight, kept calling us back.

Shortly after Doug was diagnosed, I started having recurring dreams that I accurately referred to as nightmares. Each version varied in some details, but all took place in the ocean and provided the same plotline. These night trips to the ocean were juxtaposed with my lived, life-giving experiences at the beach. Each dream began with Doug and me together, familiarly enjoying the water. Abruptly, everything would change. A hurricane or tsunami would engulf us. As soon as I would get both of us standing, then we'd both be down again. I was exhausted and gasping for breath, knowing one or both of us were not going to get out alive. I then awoke in terror. The nightmares were so tangible and dreadful.

I didn't have to be Carl Jung to attempt an interpretation. My dreams mirrored my reality. Our lives were abruptly upended. We were in the midst of a storm, clinging to each other. Each violent wave paralleled the waves of emotions and information that came at us in our waking lives. It felt like we were being dragged under rapidly, with no time to catch our breath or process. Worst of all, I couldn't save Doug from this experience. Would either or neither of us survive?

I've always been fascinated by my dreams. I knew through my dreams that my subconscious was trying to help me come to terms with what was happening. I was advised to consider that perhaps my spirit guides were speaking to me through my dreams, enlightening me, guiding me. Whether through my subconscious or spirit guides, I was offered insights and invited to learn the lessons from my dream life. These troubling dreams would recur until I took note of the signs and symbols and responded to their meaning and message.

The first obvious insight from these dreams was that they afforded a look into my subconscious and made visible that which hadn't yet surfaced in my conscious state. This time was too soon after the diagnosis and still too traumatic for me to begin processing it all at once. With guidance, I began to adjust, to integrate, to move forward. The recurring dreams ceased over time.

It was later in our journey that the real and lasting message of the dreams came to me. The ocean was an analogy for our lives. Ocean waves break at the shore. They beat and slap the surface. Despite storms and turmoil and noise on the surface of the water, if you go deep, you will find it is calm and peaceful and still.

Appropriately, my friend shared this Tibetan teaching/meditation with me:

> The ocean has waves, yet the ocean is not particularly disturbed by them. Waves will rise and go back into the ocean. Be like the ocean looking at its own waves. Whatever thoughts and emotions arise, allow them to rise and settle, like the waves in the ocean. Let go and the wave's crest will carry you to unknown shores. Let it all go and find a deep place of rest and peace and a certain transformation.

The message was clear, and the takeaway was real. I needed to surrender and do a deep dive to go into the depths of my being, deep into my inner strength and wisdom. Meditation, mindfulness, and deep breathing facilitated the peaceful process for me. As the familiar hymn reminded me, "No storm can shake my inmost calm."

DONNA BROWN BENTON

DONNA BROWN BENTON

Quandary with Questions

INQUIRING MINDS WANT to know how it first occurred to me that Doug might have cognitive issues. I can cite the exact time and place. School had just ended for the school year, and our family headed to Disney World for our much anticipated vacation. Upon awakening to our hotel's automated call the first morning, Doug kissed me and asked me what day it was. I thought that was a strange question coming from him, but I simply said, "Tuesday."

He then asked, "What time does the shuttle leave?"

My answer, "9:20."

He went into the bathroom to shower while I stayed in bed, waiting my turn. When he came out of the bathroom, he asked me those same two questions. I calmly responded with the same two answers, but I was flipping out inside. *What day is it?* Doug never had to ask that question. Never. He was the most exacting, left-brained, detail-oriented person I'd ever encountered. By contrast, I am abstract, random, and slow on sensory details. I always tease that if I started with dementia, no one would notice the difference. With Doug, I couldn't help but notice.

Doug's recurring questions were a preview of coming attractions. Recurring questions are a hallmark of dementia. That fact took some getting used to. I simply couldn't fathom that an adult as bright and engaged as Doug either couldn't remember the answer I'd just shared or, worse, didn't remember that he'd already asked the same question multiple times.

I'm a patient person by nature, but even a patient person can eventually lose it. I understand, but I still cringe when I watch people interact with dementia folks by screaming at them like they have an inability to hear the answer given the first time. More painful is watching them humiliate the person by telling them, "I already told you ten times!"

Luckily for Doug and me, one of his wise and wonderful doctors shared an image that kept me from responding in the same frantic manner. He told me to visualize Doug's brain as a cassette tape recorder with no tape inside. If there's no tape, no matter how loudly you scream, nor how many times you repeat it, it won't record in Doug's brain.

Armed with this image and my deep commitment to always honor Doug, I answered each of his questions like it was the first time he'd asked because, for him, it was. To keep this up, I challenged myself with a creative mind game. My plan was that, no matter how many times he repeated a question, I would respond each time in a uniquely different way to communicate the same answer.

A cassette recorder is a dated visual, but it came just in time for both Doug and me. Love is patient. Love is kind.

Pop Quizzes

SOME OF MY worst memories of my school days were pop quizzes, especially when I hadn't read the chapter or was otherwise completely unprepared. I hated the feeling of knowing I would fail. How humiliating! Who likes being called on in class when you don't have your hand up and you have no clue of the answer?

No wonder Doug dreaded the Mini-Mental status tests he'd have to take at the beginning of every medical office visit. Since the questions were always the same, Doug would ask me to practice with him in the car all the way to the various appointments. "Who is the current president?" and "What month is it?" and on and on through all the questions that would be on the test. I knew the rehearsal would be for naught during the test, but I was happy to offer support every time he asked. The outcome was always the same; he'd only be able to answer some correctly and, eventually, none. During the process, he'd look anxiously toward me, his face begging for help, which I very much wanted to give but obviously couldn't.

As much as I hated the whole process, I understood why this standardized test is necessary in the medical world. However, I believe that clinical tests should be limited to the clinical setting.

Our family and friends were unquestionably supportive. No pop quizzes. "Do you remember …?" or "What is the name of …?" Instead, we all worked to relieve his bewilderment and prompted him to alleviate his embarrassment. "Doug, I know you remember meeting …, my work colleague." "Doug, look at this great picture from our special trip to Hawaii." No pop quizzes, no failure, no shame. You can relax. We have your back.

I Still Know Him

OF ALL THE difficult questions asked, the one that caused me the most consternation was, "Does Doug still know you?" It was the most frequently asked question. Without supportive data, I am confident it is the most frequently asked question of everyone with a loved one with dementia. It was the question I was both asked the most and hated the most. Who wants to think you're a stranger to your beloved, your spouse, your partner, your parent, the person you're loving and for whom you're caring? To know and be known is a deep human need.

It seems in our culture that we use the answer to this question as a real point of demarcation in dementia. I know firsthand of a family whose young mother had early-onset dementia. Her attending physician told the family they should prepare themselves as she would not know them by Christmas. Once the person with dementia crosses this perceived mark, it's as if everything changes. Our judgments of the quality of their life, our relationship with them, and the feelings for the need to visit and spend quality time with them all shift.

I struggled each time I was asked this question. I sought to resolve this dilemma through reflection on my own experience with Doug and in dialogue with my holistic counselor and others.

I came to the realization that there is a difference between knowledge and knowing. It didn't matter to me that cognitively Doug no longer knew my name was Donna or realized that I was his wife. What mattered to both of us was that there was still a knowing of my energy, of my presence, of my love. There was still a knowing of my spirit and soul. This knowing was confirmed each time he'd reach for my hand or smile at me. We still shared thirty-five years of knowing each other and sharing life together, even if he couldn't recall the memories or facts of it.

But questions from others continued. "Does Doug still know you?" My experience with him and our shared spiritual connection made it easier to answer. Confidently, I responded, "I believe he does, and as importantly, I still know him."

Doug granted me his last gift of knowing at suppertime of the very night he went into a coma. When I came home from work, he greeted me nonverbally with his final luminous smile and his tight, knowing, loving hug.

I know this is a tough time of year for you but, I think about Doug and the twinkle in his eyes when you would come home from work. 🌷

Sent from Yahoo Mail on Android

Oh my. It's so good to hear from you. I think of you and Doug often. I've told your love story several times. The day before he went into a coma, he had such a great day. You came home that day, hugged and kissed him and he got tears in his eyes.

These two email excerpts that I received after Doug's death from his caregiver illustrate his still knowing me.

DONNA BROWN BENTON

Matters of the Heart

SOMETIME EARLY IN the first year of living with the reality and long-suffering of Doug's future, I realized my heart was broken figuratively. I began to wonder if my heart was broken physically as well. Externally, I was still functioning fine and seemingly holding it all together. Internally, I was inconsolable. I felt I couldn't let Doug, our daughters, or even myself know the depth of my sadness.

But each Monday through Friday morning, I got in my car and turned on Anne Murray singing, "Lord, I hope this day is good." Alone in the dark, I'd cry for the entire half-hour drive to school. Upon arrival, I'd park and attempt to pull myself together quickly on the short walk into the building. From 7:30 a.m. to 2:30 p.m., I was determined to be the dedicated teacher I had always been. After any faculty meeting or after-school activities had concluded, I'd repeat the process of reflection and crying on the way home.

At some point, the trauma wasn't just emotional. I was sensing physical symptoms as well. Intermittently, but with increasing frequency, I was experiencing chest pains and numbness in my left arm. Many a night, I'd lie awake and wonder and worry about having a heart attack. Should I go to the emergency room or ignore it and hope it goes away? I knew there was a strong link between emotional and physical health. I have learned that the state of your mind has a lot to do with the state of your physical health. I had been attending caregiver seminars and was learning that the prevalence of stress was higher for the caregiver than for the person with dementia. The stakes heightened when I learned the statistics of the caregiver dying before the person with dementia. I absolutely could not die. Who would take care of Doug and our daughters?

My symptoms raged on. Were they caused by stress, or were they an indication that I was having a heart attack? During yet another sleepless night, I decided I had to resolve this. I simply couldn't go on this way. I had to know. I had to get medical help for my heart if that was indicated. If these recurring symptoms were induced by stress, I would be free. I could drop this terrible extra burden of worry I was carrying.

In the morning, I called in sick, got the girls off to school, and got Doug off to adult daycare. Before I lost my nerve to follow through, I started randomly calling cardiology practices. After several refusals, I finally reached the office of a doctor who could see me later that afternoon. Miraculously, his office also accepted my health insurance and was located relatively close to our home.

Until it was time to leave for the appointment, through the drive there, and in the waiting room, the time was filled with fear. Finally, the wait was over. A large, gentle octogenarian walked in. He greeted me warmly and put me at ease. He invited me to share my story in response to the usual inquiry, "What brings you in today?" I delivered my rehearsed monologue about Doug's diagnosis resulting in my soaring stress level and physical symptoms. I ended with the goal of needing to know if I was having a heart attack or not. The cardiologist applauded my coming, agreed that I needed a definitive answer, and said the first step would be an electrocardiogram (EKG). He left the room, and the technician came in with the EKG machine. It took longer to put all the probes in place than it did to complete the actual test. Shortly after, the doctor returned. He was holding the long paper feed, peering at me over the results. He calmly said, "I'm afraid you may have already had a heart attack." He pointed to the troubling bleeps, but they meant nothing to me. "I'm going to write you a note for a medical leave from teaching until we get you diagnosed and well."

He scheduled the next test, a treadmill stress test, for a few days later. I teased that I'd flunk a stress test even if my heart was fine. My heart flunked the test. The following few weeks were filled with scheduling the next test, waiting to be called with the findings from the last test, and then scheduling another test. That's what was happening physically. Emotionally, I was freaking out, facing Doug's mortality, and now, secretly, my own.

Doug accompanied me to each subsequent appointment. He was unusually quiet and pale, his telltale signs that he was deeply troubled. I wasn't certain how much he was grasping what was happening, but we definitely were both experiencing reciprocal love and worry. Both of us were tormented by the what-ifs for the other.

To be conclusive, the doctor determined I needed to have a heart catheterization. The results would be definitive and determine any blockage. I was well prepared for the sobering outcome of the heart cath. I could be facing open-heart surgery. When it was time to leave Doug in the waiting room and be wheeled in for the procedure and uncertain outcome, neither of us had words. Both had lots of tears during a long embrace.

I was braced for the worst but got the best outcome I could have hoped or prayed for. What was presenting as an irregularity on all the previous tests was actually regular for me. I had not had a heart attack. In fact, all my arteries were clear, no blockage. The doctor was as surprised and relieved as I was. He told me to take a heart attack off my list of things I had to worry about. This great news wasn't just speculation. It was clinical validation I could trust. What an incredible blessing for the entire duration of our dementia journey.

If I'm being transparent, the stress continued to ebb and flow, so the symptoms did as well. But now, I was empowered with the certitude that I was not having a heart attack. I knew I didn't need to go to the ER. I could manage the symptoms with massage therapy, deep breathing, and rest.

I continued to follow up with this dedicated doctor. Professionally, I couldn't have been in better hands than with this wise, experienced cardiologist. Personally, he always inquired as to how both my husband and I were doing as Doug's Alzheimer's progressed.

Upon Doug's death, of course, new grief-related heart symptoms developed. I needed another dose of reassurance, and I returned to my safe space. Just being in this doctor's presence was calming. We talked. The tech did the usual EKG. The doctor listened to my heart and lungs. All checked out again. I thanked him profusely, and we said our goodbyes. He started to leave the room, stopped, turned toward me, and shared a final prognosis. "Donna, when your heart heals emotionally, it will heal physically as well." That proved to be clinically correct.

DONNA BROWN BENTON

Serving and Being Served

I T WAS 1969. Though my path had not yet crossed with Doug's, we later discovered that we were both living in Cincinnati at the same time. I was in college and peacefully protesting the Vietnam War. Doug was also in college and determining his future regarding the same war. The Selective Service System was about to initiate lotteries to issue draft numbers determining the order of call to military service. Doug anguished over the difficult decision with all the known and unknown implications. He finally determined he would temporarily stop pursuing his college degree and enlist in the U.S. Army. He reported for duty in September 1969. He completed his active duty and subsequent Army Reserve service in 1975.

Doug and I met and began dating ten years after his enlistment. In our early getting-to-know-you conversations, Doug shared with me that he was an army veteran and the various bases where he had been stationed. His parents gave me pictures of his younger self in military uniform taken at various times throughout his tour of duty. After we were married and were visiting my sister's family in Colorado, Doug took me to Fort Carson to show me where he was stationed for a time.

Once when I had pneumonia, Doug shared with me his army pneumonia story. During the morning roll call, he was so weak and sick that he passed out, fell out of formation, and regained consciousness in the base infirmary.

Except for these occasional glimpses into that formative period of Doug's life, I remained on the outside looking into his army experience. I respected Doug's reluctance to talk about it as often as I would have liked. I assumed it was "standard operating procedure" for some veterans; my father also shared very little of his army experience during World War II. Sometimes the deepest feelings express themselves in silence.

Doug's honorable discharge status as a veteran lay dormant for twenty-five years, from 1975 to 2000. The new millennium was the first point of reconnection for Doug and the Department of Veterans Affairs (VA). We decided we needed to access the veteran medical benefits for which Doug was eligible in order to begin a new search for diagnosis and treatment. We had spent two full years attempting to meet this target in the private medical sector using Doug's health insurance. This yielded no diagnosis, only exclusions. We were anxious; time was passing, and

Doug's symptoms were slowly progressing. With persistence, fueled by our increasing discouragement, we completed the lengthy application process. We waited. What a relief when the letter of acceptance arrived. Doug's Veterans Affairs medical benefits were activated. Doug could receive healthcare services at the Louisville VA.

To get started as soon as possible, we began as a walk-in at Dupont Medical Health Clinic, arriving in the afternoon on New Year's Eve, shortly before the early closing time. It was obvious no one working that day was thrilled to see us show up close to their closing, but they didn't let it affect the way we were treated, either personally or professionally. The attending intake physician assistant was empathetic to both Doug and to me. He shared that he was subbing for someone that day and wasn't happy about it until he met us and heard our story. He wanted to help us and promised he could and would. He recommended we wait as long as it might take to get an initial appointment with his recommended doctor. That doctor's areas of expertise were in both neurology and psychiatry. We agreed and left encouraged. If that day's experience was a preview of coming attractions, we had made the right decision. VA Medical Center was the right place to turn.

The recommended doctor who headed Doug's medical team worked with one of his medical school professors who, in turn, provided the long-awaited diagnosis. Over the course of the next decade, all of Doug's medical needs were met. He received high-quality and comprehensive care from all of the medical personnel in his Purple Primary Care Clinic, at the hospital as an inpatient and outpatient and in the emergency room.

When Doug was no longer mobile, VA Medical Center continued the same level of care, as all services transitioned to home-based for the next four years. VA Medical Center also provided all the medical equipment and a custom-built wheelchair to accommodate his above-average height as well as a Hoyer lift to get him in and out of bed and chairs and off the floor after falls. Doug was provided all his prescription medicine. Without VA Medical Center, we would never have been able to provide for all of Doug's needs. Upon enrollment, they promised in writing to do their best to provide Doug with healthcare second to none. Mission accomplished! Throughout, every VA Medical Center professional who interacted with Doug would sincerely thank him for his service. Issuing Doug an honorable discharge was not the end of their distinctions. They continued to honor him through all their caring for him with dignity and respect.

Beginning his adulthood by enlisting in the army enabled Doug to close his life being cared for by the VA healthcare services. This full-circle experience fills me with reverence and wonder and thanks. At the beginning of this journey, who could have asked or imagined how it would evolve and end? Every November, Veterans Day takes on a deeper meaning and is commemorated in our home.

All that Doug experienced in and because of the army—postponing college, leaving home and loved ones, years of service—all worked for his good. His giving transformed into receiving. Initially, he served, and now, he was being served. It all worked together for Doug's good and the good of our family.

Discover true teamwork in healthcare

Program Director
Psychologist
Dietician
Wound Care RN
Primary Nurse RN
Pharmacist
Nurse Care Manager
(Physicians & Nurse Practitioners)
Social Worker
-Physical Therapist
-Occupational Therapist
-Recreational Therapist

DONNA BROWN BENTON

Teaming Up

WHEN I REFLECT on where Doug and I started his medical care journey and where we landed, I'm in awe and disbelief. We began with our family doctor, a general practitioner. In that initial visit, the doctor thought perhaps it was Alzheimer's but didn't feel he was qualified to definitively diagnose or treat. We were referred to specialist after specialist. "See a psychologist; his cognitive issues could be caused by depression." "See an endocrinologist; perhaps his thyroid is the cause." Each specialist ruled out one possible cause but failed to diagnose. This is no longer the case, but at the time of Doug's search for a diagnosis, the only way to be definitive about Alzheimer's was an autopsy of the brain. Our health insurance denied approval for a diagnostic PET scan. The search continued because no doctor could believe this healthy fifty-year-old man with no family history was presenting with Alzheimer's.

Our next move was from the private medical system to choosing to receive healthcare services at the Louisville VA Medical Center. Neither Doug nor I had ever experienced a physician-led, team-based model of care. Perhaps it was beginner's luck, but we ended up winning the trifecta of true teamwork. VA Medical Center made up our primary team, and we also had the Alzheimer's Disease Center Clinical Core at Indiana University and our Hosparus Health team, the provider of hospice services, during the end stage of Doug's illness. These three teams addressed Doug's various care needs with coordinated efforts among multiple care providers across different settings. This caused me to reflect on the old idiom, two heads are better than one.

Each brought specialized medical knowledge, wisdom, and experience to Doug's health condition. There were shared goals but clearly delineated roles. Effective communication held this all together and allowed it to work well within each agency and across all three agencies. Doug received best practices, comprehensive treatments, and high-quality care.

VA Medical Center provided the most comprehensive team. We had a physician-led holistic team of a nurse, a psychologist, a social worker, physical and occupational therapists, a dietician, and a pharmacist. Specialists were added to the team on an as-needed basis. At every appointment, each of these areas was addressed and findings reflected in a written summary. We met with various team members as appropriate. Doug and I were considered members of the team and were actively engaged and consulted about ongoing goals and changing care needs.

There were endless practical benefits to this comprehensive team approach. VA Medical Center was a one-stop shop for us. Since I was still working full-time, it meant less time off work taking Doug to various appointments all over the city. That was also a benefit for Doug as his mobility decreased. We also didn't have to be referred to other doctors and wait to be seen as a new patient. Each member of the team had access to all of Doug's medical records and easily communicated with other members. When we needed in-patient services, and when we frequented the emergency room, it was all in the same system and same location. There were no gaps or starting from scratch. All body systems are related, and one medication or method or treatment may affect another, making this centralized, shared approach critical.

Indiana University Medical Center is a renowned Alzheimer's healthcare provider. Their Alzheimer's Disease Research Center (ADRC) Clinical Core is on the leading edge of Alzheimer's research. After each appointment, the Clinical Core physician would send a summary report to Doug's doctor at VA Medical Center. This two-way communication was invaluable for seamless care. Doug never resisted going to endless appointments or treatments. Quite the contrary, he liked all the medical personnel on all three of his teams. He felt known and cared for and supported. We trusted his life to them. They felt like a family surrounding us with physical and emotional help and healing. As Doug's advocate, I couldn't be more grateful. The strength of his team was each individual member. The strength of each individual member was the team. The whole was greater than the sum of the parts.

After our profound team-based experiences, it pains me to see dementia patients struggling without all the wisdom and comprehensive resources a team-based approach afforded us. When I encounter deprived dementia patients, I suggest, refer, and do whatever I can to assist them in accessing more effective team-based care. The number of dementia patients is on the rise. I hope physician-led teams will also rise up to meet them. Dementia patients and their families need coordinated care and deserve it.

love
is all you need.

DONNA BROWN BENTON

Love Is All You Need

WHEN DOUG AND I were considering marriage, we paused at the solemnity of promising love forever. Neither of us questioned the other's potential commitment. It was an individual, internal search of wondering at our own ability to promise to love another for the rest of our lives.

At different times, we each emerged ready for vowed love. Pivotal in the process was our personal belief and experience that we can love because we are first loved. As an expression of this, we prefaced our marriage vows with the phrase, "Because of God's promise of fidelity to us, I promise fidelity to you." And continued, "I will be true to you both in good times and bad, in sickness and in health. I will love you and reverence you all the days of my life."

Our wedding was a sincere and wholehearted expression of love, but actions are the authentic manifestations of love. Our romantic love had to ascend to agape love.

Upon Doug's diagnosis, I returned to my vowed promise to love unconditionally, even in bad times. I was rooted in love and motivated exclusively by my love for Doug and my relationship with him. No experience was necessary to live out this commitment, but love was a prerequisite. I often mused that the Beatles were correct: "All you need is love." Andrew Lloyd Webber expounds, "Love, love changes everything: how you live and how you die …. Love will never ever let you be the same."

The biblical characteristics of love call out and accurately align with the qualities needed to companion another on an Alzheimer's journey.

> Love is always patient and kind; love is always ready to hope and endures whatever comes.
> Love does not come to an end.
>
> (1 Corinthians 13: 4, 7)

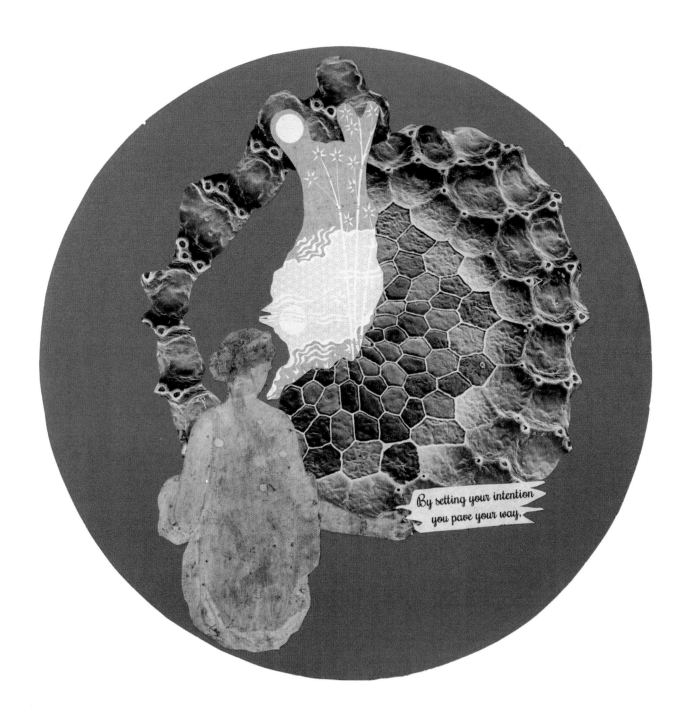

By setting your intention
you pave your way.

DONNA BROWN BENTON

Deciding and Doing

DECIDING. WHEN PEOPLE come to know Doug's Alzheimer's story, colleagues, strangers, and friends alike often ask me some version of the same probing question. It's the counterintuitive question posed in the old African teaching, "run to the roar." Friends ask, "Didn't you want to run away/ leave him? Why did you decide to stay?"

My answer is simple. I made that decision to stay two decades ago. Doug and I wrote our marriage vows together to accurately express our commitment to each other. Through different words, but with the same meaning, we promised each other unconditional love. We vowed to "run to the roar" in sickness and in health, for better or worse.

In the first almost twenty years of marriage following that promise, we found that loving unconditionally is possible but not easy. Only the beginning was easy; later, feelings of love and lust and longing waxed and waned.

We went through the stages and struggles that are predictable in marriage, but throughout, we maintained our communication and commitment. We continued to forgive, to renew, and to grow together. Our relationship strengthened.

When Doug's roar sounded, my decisive, unconditional love responded. It enabled me to instinctively and instantly run toward him. Once again, only the beginning was easy. I grew weary, and my motivation waxed and waned during some stages and situations. It was during those times that I would return to my initial decision and remember my "why." That would enable me to decide again what I had decided before.

In *The Vacationers*, Emma Straub describes it this way:

There is nothing in life harder or more important than agreeing every morning to stay the course, to go back to your forgotten self of so many years ago and to make the same decision.

I was able to decide and keep deciding for Doug. I experienced the universe rising up to meet me and empower me.

Doing. After probing questions about deciding for Doug, the next round of inquiries and comments were, "How did you do it? I never could have managed!" These were logical follow-up inquiries. After the deciding, the doing must follow.

Before I learned and practiced intention setting, implementation was not my strong suit. Many of my decisions never came to fruition. Intending to do something is not the same as setting an intention.

My initial intentions committed to paper

When I saw how sloppily I had written my intentions for caring for Doug, it brought home to me the mess of my internal self at the time. Regardless, they worked. These intentions served as the "what" and the "how" flowing from my decision. Setting these intentions ignited my motivation and determined my aligned actions. Posting them in view and often reviewing them kept me on track.

In retrospect, I am filled with peace by the correlation between what I decided to do for Doug and what I was actually able to do for Doug.

In Matilda, Roald Dahl writes, "She believed she could, so she did." My application for our situation was, "I decided I would, so I did."

DONNA BROWN BENTON

I am
his rock

his Alzheimer's caregiver

his guardian

his advocate

his voice

DONNA BROWN BENTON

Giving Care

CAREGIVING WAS THE first job responsibility I ever took on without applying or being formally prepared. Being a novice, I had a very limited concept of what I was undertaking. I had never been close to anyone living with Alzheimer's. I had a steep learning curve ahead of me. As an educator, I learned that knowledge is power. I committed to being a lifelong learner. I attended seminars, read literature to educate myself about Alzheimer's, consulted medical professionals, and networked to learn all I could as rapidly as I could.

How deeply I was committed to Doug would influence how I now cared for him. This became my first foundational aspect of caregiving for my husband. I envisioned a hybrid model. I desired to integrate my role of wife with my simultaneous role of caregiver. I intended to have my giving of care flow from our marriage. I wanted Doug to view my service as unconditional love for him in action. I viewed it as ministering to him.

Just how comprehensive my responsibility was started to become clearer as the cluster of dementia symptoms started showing up. New behaviors seemed to emerge, and new facets exhibited between each medical consultation. At each visit, I'd ask the same question of Doug's doctor. Was a newly emerging behavior or symptom caused by or connected to Doug's dementia diagnosis? Finally, on one occasion, partially as an answer to my latest inquiry and partially from frustration, the doctor blurted out, "DONNA, the answer to this question is always going to be yes, they are related. Alzheimer's originates in the brain, but the symptoms are not limited to the brain or memory loss." My nonmedical takeaway was that everything in the body begins in the brain. The doctor ended with, "This is why our treatment is holistic, and your response must be comprehensive as well." This was the whole picture I hadn't yet acquired but needed to moving forward. My caregiver job description quickly expanded exponentially.

Traditionally, the model of caregiving was limited to physical health and dealt mainly with dispensing meds and getting patients fed. It was more about managing only the patient's diagnosis and physical needs as opposed to caring for the whole person living with dementia.

As my starting point for caregiving, I also began with Doug's physical health. Those needs were concrete, practical, and immediate. The physical is the area people tend to share advice about and the area covered most often in the literature. It involves managing all things medical, from appointments to pharmaceutical issues.

For the next stage of expanding my caregiving mindset, I drew on my work responsibility supporting health education for our public school system. Health curricula are no longer only about physical health. In addition, and as importantly, holistic health focuses on social, emotional, and mental health. The whole person is treated.

Doug's emotional health was probably the most natural and most rewarding aspect of my compassionate care. The established patterns in our relationship deepened through continual verbal and nonverbal communication, encouragement, and support.

Socially, I was committed to making certain Doug could maintain his relationships and involvement, as able, at each stage. We continued celebrating birthdays and holidays and inviting family and friends to our home to interact with Doug. We continued to enjoy our favorite activities, such as listening to music, attending concerts and the theater, and traveling as long as possible.

Addressing Doug's mental health involved assisting him in maintaining his independence and dignity as long as possible. We worked on managing stress and depression and keeping him stimulated and productive.

Spiritually, I assisted Doug with maintaining his purpose, nourishing his spirit, and continuing our spiritual practices. Of paramount importance was recognizing that his essence was persisting despite his physical and mental diminishment.

All of these aspects of health remained constant needs throughout. The fluid nature of the progression, however, called for constant reevaluation and determination of how each need could somehow continue to be specifically met.

In addition to all of these aspects of comprehensive caregiving, my overarching role was being an advocate for Doug, as he was no longer able to advocate for himself. I was his voice, pleading on his behalf, navigating complicated systems for his health and welfare while assuring his needs were being met. I was grateful I was able to fill this role for Doug. From this experience, I became convinced that every person living with dementia needs an advocate.

While Doug was still able to express his deep gratitude through words, he did. Later, his thank-you was delivered through a smile and a knowing nod. In the book of blessings he kept throughout, at some point, he simply wrote *DONNA* in all caps as entry number nineteen. Later, he drew a long arrow moving me up above number one. He was always number one in my book as well.

DONNA BROWN BENTON

The Long Goodbye

I HATE GOODBYES. I'VE always said of myself that I can't part with a pen that is out of ink. How was I going to live through this imminent parting with Doug? Sitting down with Mike Wallace of CBS's *60 Minutes*, Nancy Reagan first described Ronald's Alzheimer's as the "long, long goodbye." Nancy's description resonated with audiences and came to characterize Alzheimer's. Somehow, in usage, the phrase got shortened to just the "long goodbye." It's not always long in measured months or years but long in ongoing losses, each loss requiring a goodbye by both the person and their loved one. I initially described my long goodbye with Doug as falling off a cliff in slow motion. That description seemed accurate at the time—the trajectory downward, the outcome determined, and the timing undetermined. Part of me wanted the freefall to be long. I didn't want it to be over quickly because then Doug would be gone and our time together ended. Another part of me couldn't continue to live each day only focusing on losses and goodbyes.

This internal struggle invited me to start thinking about how relative time is. How long is a long goodbye? Somehow, out of my long-term memory, I pulled out Einstein's theory of relativity: the rate at which time passes depends upon your frame of reference. My mind continually makes connections. It instantly went from Einstein's rate of time passing to James Taylor singing, "The secret of life is enjoying the passage of time … But since we're on our way down, we might as well enjoy the ride." He continues, "Now the thing about time is that time isn't really real. It's just your point of view." Could Doug and I adopt the point of view of enjoying the ride down?

Enter Doug's psychologist. He insisted that happy memories last longer than sad ones. Based on that reality and the relativity of time, he encouraged us to front-load Doug's ride down with pleasure and many positive experiences. Doing so could help extend the early stages longer and help the end stages be shorter. We were excited to take the doctor's advice and begin living as prescribed. At Doug's request, we started with a visit to the Rock & Roll Hall of Fame and continued with a variety of life-giving experiences for as long as Doug was able.

My new frame of reference slowly shifted. I went from feeling like we were falling off a cliff in slow motion to feeling like Doug was living with Alzheimer's, not dying with it. That meant life and loss were both real and able to coexist. Throughout, we strove for a life balance of holding on and letting go, of beginnings and endings, embracing life until there was only the death of Doug's physical self. Ironically, our long goodbye was not long enough.

The present moment is filled with joy and happiness. If you are attentive, you will see it.

Life is a gift... enjoy and bask in every moment you are in.

CELESTINE CHUA

Today

DONNA BROWN BENTON

Carpe Diem

DEMENTIA GETS A bad rap. It's known for all losses, no gains. Surprisingly, Alzheimer's offered Doug and me the great lesson of living in the present. This progressive disease brought us exclusively to life in the present. Initially, Doug's short-term memory faded. Over time, his long-term memory faded as well. His past was gone. His future was unavailable to him. Doug lived contentedly in the present. As I watched him, I was called to meet him in his "now-ness."

Doug was always more of a present-tense person than I ever would be. Before his diagnosis, I spent most days remembering and treasuring the past and planning for and looking forward to what would happen in the future. Doug's diagnosis abruptly changed my MO. The past we shared before his diagnosis was now history. Despite my pleas to get our old life back, our past would never be present again. Trying to flee to the future offered no solace either. I couldn't wish it away nor fast-forward through it. Our future looked only worrisome and inhospitable to me. It was the definition of *anxiety*—fear of an unknown future that often doesn't play out as feared.

So by some combination of choice and force, the present was all we had. Our past is over, and tomorrow never comes. The present is the only place life is lived. We had an illustrative example of this truth amid Doug's experience. Doug made a recurring request to travel to Oregon to visit his brother. We were finally able to arrange the trip's dates with his brother, and since Doug was traveling alone, we coordinated safety procedures with the airline. Doug's sequencing skills with dates and times were diminishing. He was continuously asking, "When am I going? How much longer?"

At last, the time had arrived for his long-awaited trip. Doug and I kept in touch via phone each night. I could tell from the excitement in his voice that he was having a wonderful week. In the background, his family coaxed him to describe the events they'd shared. Making music with his brother was the highlight of the trip. Clearly, he was fully living and loving life in the present.

Shortly after he returned home, he again began asking when he was going to visit his brother. It was painful to hear and harder to believe his short-term memory was gone. He couldn't recall recently being in Oregon. But in truth, it didn't matter. In the present, the visit was real and life-giving for Doug.

Without realizing it, Doug modeled for me how to live in the present. I began by slowly relinquishing my habit of multitasking. Though doing two things at once seemed time-saving, I realized I was not present for either task. I yielded to intentionally paying attention to the here and now, to my thoughts and feelings, my sensations and surroundings. It was a reminder to stop and smell the proverbial roses.

Another area of growth I needed to master for present-tense living was to drop my judgment and evaluations and accept the present on its own terms. My constant mantra became "It is what it is." Doug's dementia was not deemed good or bad—it just was. I kept repeating the first principle of the serenity prayer: "to accept the things I cannot change," to be content with what was and could not be changed.

Through our early years together, Doug and I shared a love for the movie *Dead Poets Society*. Our takeaway from the movie was the phrase *carpe diem*. We had incorporated this into our vernacular and used it to mean, "Let's do this day with gusto." The actual translation is "seize the day." By definition, it's used to urge someone to make the most of the present time and give little thought to the future. Alzheimer's challenged us to seize the day. Alzheimer's gave us the gift of sixteen years of todays.

DONNA BROWN BENTON

Flower Power

UNLIKE SOME GROOMS, Doug was actively involved in the planning and execution of our wedding. We worked together on most of the decisions and details of our wedding day including the venues, our gift registry, liturgy planning, and writing our vows, just to mention a few. The only exception was meeting with the florist. Doug was meeting with his band at the same time, rehearsing to play our reception. My dear friend and bridesmaid was drafted as my partner in picking our flowers. Roberta had a favorite florist, so that's where we headed one Saturday morning. We spent half the day exploring and eliminating flower choices. When designing and creating for any special event, I care greatly about every visual detail. Most importantly, everything must be color-coordinated. I had chosen shades of burgundy for our December wedding. After all the time spent consulting with the florist, I was still having trouble closing off my options and making the difficult decisions. I relied on my accompanying friend for her input. She recommended I choose Stargazer lilies for my bridal bouquet. She convincingly pointed out the cranberry markings decorating each white petal. She closed her persuasive case by assuring me they were beautiful, would make a statement, and would photograph well. I was thrilled I had her sub for Doug at the floral appointment.

I fell in love with Stargazer lilies on our wedding day, and they forever remind me of that special day.

On our fifth wedding anniversary, Doug surprised me by having the florist send me an arrangement of Stargazer lilies. I was touched that he remembered that they'd made up my bridal bouquet and that he carried that memory with him for five years. What a romantic husband! What a memorable anniversary! That occasion marked these lilies transitioning from our wedding flower to our marriage flower. They not only played an important part in our wedding day but also continued to be meaningful in our marital relationship. They became a visual symbol of our love and commitment. We sent them to, or received them from, one another on various birthdays and anniversaries. We sometimes bought them as bouquets at our grocery store on a mundane Monday. When we were entertaining, they sometimes adorned our dinner table as a centerpiece. Most often, their place of honor was in our bedroom, atop Doug's dresser.

Some of our friends and family started supporting what they teasingly called our flower fetish. I resisted the term *fetish*, until I learned that another definition is "an object worshipped because it is considered to be inhabited by a spirit." That definition fit perfectly. Stargazers started showing up everywhere. Friends would text pictures from wherever they were when they spotted our flowers. A former student of mine, who became our hair stylist many years later, got in on the trend. Kristi's clients would sometimes send her flowers, and often the arrangements contained Stargazers. Luckily for us, she was allergic to them and couldn't tolerate their scent. To this day, as soon as they are delivered, she calls me with the good news. "Doug sent you flowers to the salon again. How quickly can you get here to pick them up?" What a win-win-win for her and Doug and me.

About a decade after we chose Stargazer lilies for our wedding, they were chosen in 1991 to become the floral blanket for the winning filly of the Kentucky Oaks. Lilies for the fillies! Throughout the annual Kentucky Derby season, Stargazers are a focus. Doug and I pretended all of Louisville was celebrating with us. It was meaningful to us that the Oaks race and these flowers have become a celebration of new life for breast cancer survivors.

During the progression of Doug's dementia, having flowers in our home couldn't be limited to special occasions. When someone you love has an expiration date, you have to make each day a special occasion.

Surrounding ourselves with flowers became a simple act of the prescribed self-care. Their presence brought us beauty and joy. Whatever the weather outside, it could be springtime inside our home. Each bloom promised new life as it slowly erupted. Its defined spirit spilled out and surrounded us.

Of course, I chose our marriage flowers for Doug's memorial. Stargazers continue to represent to me our eternal love. Doug, your love lives on.

WE LIVE IN THE HOUSE WE ALL BUILD

DONNA BROWN BENTON

There's No Place Like Home

SHORTLY AFTER OUR marriage, Doug and I relocated from Cincinnati, Ohio, to Louisville, Kentucky, for employment. We spent the first few years living in apartments while spending every nonworking hour looking for a house to buy. We were eager to own our first home, a nest to begin a family and raise our children. We also wanted a hospitable place for family and friends to gather, share meals, and celebrate together. Since we were newlyweds, we were long on love but short on cash. This reality put us in the market for an advertised fixer-upper. Doug was up for the renovation of our handyman special. His grandfathers were carpenters, and Doug had helped his father maintain their historic childhood home. Now it was Doug's turn. He had all the talent and tools to renovate the hundred-year-old house we finally found.

For the next fifteen years, we worked tirelessly to slowly transform this house into our home. Simultaneously and symbolically, we were building our marriage and family as well. The investment of our time, energy, and talents made our home very special to us. It became the container for our family's life story and love story. Luckily, our family had an established foundation, as everything was about to dramatically shift upon Doug's dementia diagnosis. Suddenly, instead of renovating our home and looking forward, everything stopped, and our bright future looked dark.

Would Doug be able to continue working to finish our home restoration? Would we be able to afford to pay our home mortgage without Doug's income? Of paramount concern, would Doug be able to continue living in our home through his end stage?

Without being asked, many people were quick to inform me that I would have to put Doug in a memory care home at some point. People encouraged me to start the arduous task of identifying a good nursing home, insisting this would enable me to be prepared when necessary.

Since this was all new to me, I took the advice and contacted a few recommended places and eventually made myself tour one. Even one of Doug's doctors suggested that if I was going to change Doug's living space,

I should do it sooner rather than later. He explained this would capitalize on Doug's remaining short-term memory capacity to allow him to better acclimate to new surroundings.

Initially, I just assumed all these opinions were correct and needed to be heeded. They were presented as the automatic default decision. But I kept stalling. I couldn't make peace with even the thought of placing Doug in a home. I wrestled with haunting questions. "Why couldn't I take care of Doug in our home? Since this is Doug's home also, doesn't he deserve to continue to live in the home he contributed to both financially and with his sweat equity? Everything in our home was still familiar and in his long-term memory. Could he adjust and function in an environment where everything was unfamiliar? Wouldn't the expense of a facility be cost-prohibitive, making it impossible to continue to maintain our current home for our daughters and me?"

I struggled with these issues for months. I sought counsel, weighed the alternatives, anticipated outcomes, and listened to my inner voice. Subconsciously, I was also being influenced by past role modeling of my mother around this issue. Her German-descent extended family committed to caring for their loved ones in their homes until death, and they kept their promise.

With increased clarity, I ultimately made the decision to keep Doug in our home for the duration. This was undoubtedly the most vital decision I had to make for him. Time would confirm that I made the right decision.

If I am being fully transparent, there were difficult aspects of the decision to keep him home. I struggled living with all the medical equipment of grab bars, a wheelchair and ramp, and a Hoyer lift, all filling our home environment with a clinical feel. Also, often having a daytime caregiver and other medical personnel in our home sometimes made me feel like I lived in a facility rather than our personal home. With perspective, though, these were small annoyances compared to all the blessings and benefits of having Doug with us in our dwelling from diagnosis to death.

Keeping him physically close was the antidote to all of the other losses we were experiencing. Doug was still part of our family life. Friends and family visited, and holiday celebrations continued. He enjoyed his favorite home-cooked meals and continued watching his favorite TV shows and listening to his personal music selections. Doug and I shared many hours sitting together on our front and back porches, renewed by sunshine and fresh air. His surroundings were familiar, which extended his time of fuller functioning.

While the decision for Doug to stay in our home was initially guided by what would be best for Doug, the surprise positive by-product was that it proved to be wonderful for me as well—a true win-win. At the end of my workday, I was able to return home instead of heading to a nursing home to visit. While engaging with Doug in our home, I could simultaneously keep up with daily housekeeping tasks of washing, cooking, cleaning, and more. It was our place of peace, our secret garden, our shelter from the storm.

DONNA BROWN BENTON

There were at least three givens that made this stay-at-home decision possible to implement. What a lucky fate that the home we bought when we were young had a first-floor bedroom and bath. It was a nicety then, but an absolute necessity later. Since Doug had early-onset Alzheimer's, I was still young enough and healthy enough to care for Doug. Of prime importance, the medical community, including VA Medical Center and Hosparus Health services, provided essential in-home services that made it possible. At the end stage, our daytime in-home caregiver saw us through as well.

All that Doug poured into our home came back to him. He was able to live in his home until the end. It was familiar and safe. It was a haven for him to enjoy and rest. Our first home turned out to be our forever home. We agreed with Dorothy from *The Wizard of Oz*. "There's no place like home. There's no place like home."

For Doug's memorial liturgy, we chose the theme of "Bring him home," expressed through the chosen readings, songs, and prayers.

Doug, how we wish you could have stayed with us in your earthly dwelling, but we are certain you have returned home to your source. You have returned to the home of your soul.

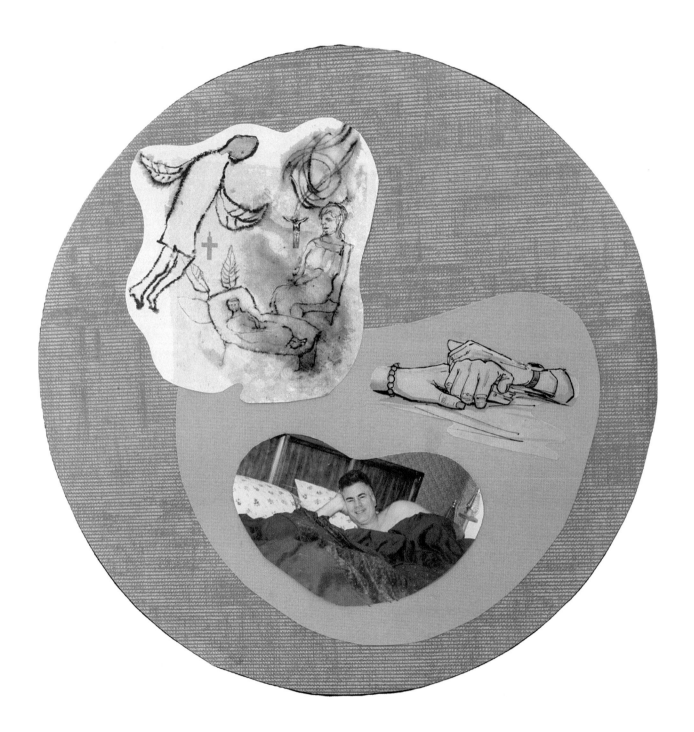

DONNA BROWN BENTON

Let Me Lay Down Beside You

ABOUT THIRTEEN YEARS into the progression of Doug's dementia, his home-based primary care medical team decided a hospital bed was becoming a necessity. His physical functioning level was declining. This change was recommended for Doug's safety, transfer, and treatment.

While the medical team was ready for immediate implementation, I sensed a wall of resistance rising in me. Negative flashbacks of each of my parents in home-hospital beds at the end of their lives were overtaking me. The same issues to be solved when my parents needed hospital beds were surfacing now in this scenario with my husband.

The only room in our home on the first floor for possible bed placement was the living room. Would taking away the use of the living room for the rest of our family be a viable option? The proximity of the living room from our bedroom was not close. Would I be able to hear and respond in a timely way to Doug's needs? The primary obstacle for me, though, was the bed rails. Admittedly, while they are needed to keep the patient in, they simultaneously keep those who love and care for them out. This was a deal-breaker for me.

While previously visiting and caring for my parents when each was terminally ill, I logged hours of presence with my arm falling asleep while draped over the railings to hold their hands. I remember barely being able to bend over the bars far enough to hug and kiss them. This was now a nonnegotiable for me with my husband. I could not choose to move Doug out of our bedroom after three decades of marriage. This would escalate the sense of loss and isolation he was experiencing. I was convinced that we needed to continue to sleep in the same bed for whatever time we had remaining.

I believe that inspiration makes you figure out what to do when you don't know what to do. The idea of replacing our queen-size bed with a queen-size hospital bed came to me as a possible solution to our dilemma. "Is there such a thing?" I wondered. After researching, I was delighted and relieved to discover such medical equipment is available. Citing cost, policy, and insurance, the two agencies servicing Doug were only able to provide us with a single hospital bed. I would not be deterred and was still determined to make this inspiration become a reality.

I honestly don't remember if I begged or borrowed the money, but somehow, I was able to make this happen. I purchased an electronic base and skirt and an accompanying queen-size mattress. Attaching this to our existing headboard concealed the clinical parts and maintained the familiar look and feel of our bedroom.

One of the many physical benefits of continuing to sleep together each night couldn't have been anticipated. Doug's decline took him through a period when he would abruptly sit up in bed and then couldn't remember how to lie back down. I was next to him and able to assist him with this and other numerous needs.

The emotional closeness proved to be the best outcome. Each night as we settled in bed, Doug would move his hand around until he found my hand to hold. Many nights, consistent sleep wasn't possible for me. During my awake time, I'd bask in the moonlight entering our tall bedside windows illuminating Doug's face. His presence would fill me with peace. Sometimes I would lay my head on his chest to feel his heartbeat and experience this life force still pulsing through him.

The gift of spending nights together was a much-needed antidote to the Alzheimer's dealings of our days. Neither of us had to *do* anything; we could just *be* together nightly for the last years of our married life.

Early in our marriage, Doug would play his guitar and sing to me John Denver's song written for his Annie. Some of the lyrics are really a request:

> Let me lay down beside you,
> Let me always be with you.
> Let me give my life to you,
> Let me die in your arms.

Perhaps on some subconscious level, this song may have been my inspiration for the queen-size hospital bed decision and implementation. These lyrics that Doug frequently sang to me in the beginning of our relationship ultimately came to fruition for him.

DONNA BROWN BENTON

DONNA BROWN BENTON

The Audacious Hope of Rooted Things

A T THE TIME of Doug's diagnosis, his doctor declared it was definitely early-onset Alzheimer's. There was also nothing hopeful in the prognosis that followed. The doctor was clear—there is no cure, no treatment, certainly not in our lifetimes. "Perhaps in time for your daughters' generation," he mumbled. He offered a drug that might slow the progression, but there would be no remissions. If this doctor's goal was to make certain we left with no false hopes, he accomplished his mission. There was nothing positive to hold onto. No gray areas.

Imagine our deep, shared despair and complete lack of hope. The only certitude was Doug's progressive diminishment and resulting death. I was certain we would feel like this permanently.

During a happenstance discussion with a mentor, I was bemoaning how hard it was to live without hope; the cause of that hopelessness was not going to change. In response, she shared with me her lived experience of "Hope." She had also struggled with hope in a similar life experience and emerged with this wisdom. In her new understanding, she related, there is a difference between *Hope* with a capital "H" and *hope* with a small "h." Think of small "h" *hope* as a noun, concrete and specific. It's wishful thinking, only what we can envision. Our wishes are a laundry list of demands for how we want things to go. Once I heard that, I mentally moved all my wishful thinking for our situation to that small "h" column. A few examples of my numerous small "h" specifics were my hope that Doug wouldn't get put in the placebo group of his Alzheimer's clinical trials and that Doug would live longer than the average eight years predicted.

She then encouraged me to think of *Hope* with a capital "H" as a verb, an action word. Doing so invites one to live in the spirit of Hope. It doesn't demand specific outcomes; it keeps one open to surprises of unforeseen eternal things that may evolve. Even though Doug still had Alzheimer's, I could preserve the presence of Hope because it is not situationally dependent. It is possible to lose hope but still maintain one's spirit of Hope. The universe is constantly conspiring for my good. I remained open to the surprising ways that Hope may come to us in the midst of this seemingly hopeless situation.

As a novice attempting to live in the spirit of Hope, nature gave me a visual gift. Right outside our bedroom, on the side of our home, a small Johnny-jump-up flower, with its lush green foliage, spontaneously germinated between cracks in the sidewalk. What a testimony to the audacious hope of this tiny, rooted thing. The flower was an example of Hope in process. It began as a seed in the darkness before it made its way to the surface, to the light. This tender flower served as motivation for me to keep pushing through our darkness and seemingly impermeable reality with Hope.

On the way in and out of our home daily, I visited my flower friend to make certain she was thriving and to remind myself to live in the spirit of Hope and to share that spirit with Doug.

DONNA BROWN BENTON

Enter Peace

DONNA BROWN BENTON

When the Student Is Ready, the Teacher Appears
(Zen Proverb)

ONE OF THE great satisfactions of my position within our urban school system was working with local community partners to promote health education and programming for our students. I collaborated for a few years with a medical doctor and his wife, who is a nurse. Besides working to improve health outcomes for our students, they initiated many healthy endeavors in our community. They, along with a psychotherapist, hosted a weekly talk radio program, *The Art of Healthy Living*. They had given me a refrigerator magnet advertising this call-in show. I posted this front and center on our home refrigerator as a reminder to tune in each Saturday morning. Each show featured a different health focus.

One particular Saturday morning, the topic was to be Alzheimer's. Knowing well my husband's current journey, the doctor and nurse asked me to share our experience with early-onset. Despite some degree of hesitancy and vulnerability, I agreed. I knew of, but had never met, the third professional on their team. His contribution was to represent mental and emotional health in their team's holistic approach. I knew by reputation that he was a licensed clinical social worker who, at the time, also facilitated support groups for the doctor's cancer patients.

I listened with great interest to the beginning half of the broadcast. The callers painted the usual stereotypical picture of dementia—octogenarians misplacing their glasses, forgetting and repeating, and losing driving privileges.

Once it was my turn on air, I began by noting that I was asked to share our experience of early-onset since my husband was diagnosed at age fifty. Instantly, I heard an audible gasp from the counselor. His immediate questions shifted the focus to me. "How are *you* doing? Are you getting support?" His unexpected inquiries touched something deep in me that quickly surfaced, as I felt care and concern coming through the phone/radio. My extroverted self wanted to respond immediately with all I had been storing so tightly inside. Luckily, I had the presence of mind to remind myself that I was being broadcast on 50,000 watts of radio and quickly shifted the focus back to the call's purpose. I don't remember much of what else I was able to share. As the hour wound down, the counselor reminded me, and all caregivers, to get support and be mindful of self-care while giving care to others.

I was shaking as I hung up. "What just happened? What did I share aloud?" I asked myself. I wasn't certain what to make of the exchange with the counselor. Over the next couple of days, I kept thinking about his admonitions for self-care and support. He made me realize how strong and self-sufficient I always try to be. I wore a self-made superwoman cape as I juggled my more than full-time employment, our home, devotion to my dear Doug, and mothering our cherished daughters. My spontaneous desire to respond so fully and immediately to a stranger via radio told me I had some unacknowledged and unmet needs.

Later that week, Doug and I were eating dinner at the kitchen table when I looked up and saw the magnet on the refrigerator staring back at me. Since I don't believe in coincidences, I decided I should call the counselor with whom I had connected over the airwaves. While I still had the courage, I got up, took the magnet off the fridge, and put it in my purse as a reminder to reach out to him the next day. As soon as I got to work in the morning, I put my keys in my purse and pulled out the magnet. With it still in my hand, my office phone rang. "This is Donna," I answered as usual.

"This is Don Vowels," the voice replied. "The radio show team gave me your number and assured me you'd be OK with me calling. Please know I am not calling to solicit your business. I've had an independent counseling practice for two decades, and I usually have more clients than I can handle. I just felt compelled to follow up with you and encourage you to get the support you need and deserve."

"Well, this was meant to be," I exclaimed. "I was set to call you at this exact moment!" The connection was complete. We set our first appointment. Appropriately, the address for his office was 911 Barret Avenue. When my GPS announced, "You have arrived at 911," I took this as a positive sign that help and healing would take place there.

The first counseling session went well; I was at ease and comfortable sharing our story. I felt seen and heard. Because of the counselor's busy schedule, we made a series of future appointments. Due to the established trajectory of dementia, my health insurance continued to authorize appointments throughout the final four years of progression. The journey was not linear; there were periods of calm and contentment as well as times of crisis. During the darkest times, I had weekly appointments. In one of these weekly sessions, I asked, alarmed, "Does this mean I'm a basket case?"

Don smiled and reassured me. "No, to the contrary," he replied. "It means you're mentally healthy enough to recognize your reality and seek the appropriate treatment for growth and support."

DONNA BROWN BENTON

The mantra of Don's practice was "enter peace." This focused work allowed me to enter peacefully into the reality of living with Doug's dementia. Each session began with my monologue bringing Don up to speed on all that had transpired since our last meeting. I received clarity, insight, and wisdom when Don reflected back to me what he'd heard. He was skilled at weaving together all the seemingly unrelated thoughts and feelings I shared into a whole meaningful message. Sometimes he would help me work through difficult decisions, sometimes brainstorm solutions, sometimes determine courses of action, and often just receive my tears and offer encouragement and assurance so I could move forward. I was strengthened and sustained and able to stay the course.

Though Doug was past the point of active participation in our sessions, he benefited from them indirectly. By putting the proverbial oxygen mask on myself first, I was able to continue to breathe life into Doug. When I was better, he was better. Everything I learned in counseling I internalized and implemented, which as a result, bore fruit for Doug as well. Through counseling with Don, Doug and I were able to forge a path of peace amid the challenges of our life dealing and living with dementia. Without Don, we probably would have just survived. With Don, we were able to thrive.

DONNA BROWN BENTON

Food for Thought

WHEN I FIRST met Doug, I quickly learned that he enjoyed good food and breaking bread with others. I marveled at how often and how much he could eat and still be as thin as he was tall. His waist measurement and inseam were both thirty-six inches. I was always envious that he was blessed with such an active metabolism, helping to convert all he was able to eat to fuel his six-foot-six body.

For our first date, Doug invited me to dinner at a local Cincinnati restaurant famous for its desserts. He picked this establishment because his favorite food groups were meats, potatoes, and desserts. Our first meal together lasted for hours as we got acquainted by sharing our stories.

Since I had always heard that the way to a man's heart is through his stomach, I wasted no time baking him one of his favorites, carrot cake, followed by a regular supply of various delectable desserts. It worked!

At the beginning of our marriage, we cooked dinner together each evening. We enjoyed experimenting with all our culinary wedding gifts of cookbooks, a wok, a fondue pot, and more. Doug greatly appreciated what I considered my slightly above-average cooking skills, gleaned from watching my mother cook and from taking food preparation courses in college while working toward my undergraduate home economics degree. Based on Doug's meal history, he considered me a master chef. His basis for comparison was his mom's meals of Hamburger Helper or liver and onions, always served with canned peas and pearl onions.

Meals in the army didn't get any better. It's a sad commentary when the best meal the army offered was officially called creamed chipped beef on toast. Like most veterans, Doug referred to it as "shit on a shingle." Before our marriage, I teased and told Doug that I would excel in one room of our home. It's no wonder he quickly picked the kitchen. So the cooking continued.

When our girls were old enough to join us at the table, we prioritized family dinners at 5:30 p.m., when their dad got home from work. Special food choices were a requirement for all holidays and family celebrations. These special meals called for what our youngest daughter, at an early age, deemed "china night." That meant we ate in the dining room instead of the kitchen and set the table with our wedding china in place of our daily dishes.

For birthdays, the honoree got to determine the menu, pick the cake, and be serenaded with many rounds of our family's three different birthday songs. For his birthday, Doug always chose Jerry's three-layer chocolate cake or Elmer's cheesecake. I made each from scratch.

After the girls and I went to bed early each night so we could get up early for school, Doug raided the pantry for his nighttime snack. He'd settle into his favorite living room chair to zone out in front of the TV. His nightly snack choices were usually any flavor of Doritos or a big bowl of freshly popped buttered popcorn. Was it any wonder that shortly after Doug passed, the automated function on Doug's recliner gave out? The repairman showed up, turned the tired chair over, and took it apart. Imagine my embarrassment and delight when out fell years of Dorito crumbs and popcorn kernels. They were happy remnants and reminders of Doug's nocturnal snack habit.

Food was the focus of many of our social events as well. We went out for dinner at restaurants or friends' homes, and we invited family and friends to dine in or cook out at our home.

As Doug continued living with Alzheimer's, food played an important role in his care for a trifecta of reasons. Providing the social context of sharing meals with family and friends was vital to combat his increasing withdrawal and social isolation. As Doug was losing many things he had always enjoyed, such as playing video games and his musical instruments, food was something he was still able to partake in and enjoy. Besides the necessary nutrients, food sustained his physical health and nourished his social and emotional well-being. Many of our friends gifted Doug with their presence and a meal, knowing what it would mean to him.

During this time, our longtime family friend proved to be the "food angel" for Doug. In her lifetime of employment, she cooked for hospital patients and for three archbishops in Louisville's archdiocese. We called her food our "manna from heaven." The last few years, Janet would spend Saturday mornings in our kitchen cooking Doug's favorite foods. Doug interacted with her from his wheelchair. It was a special bonding time with just the two of them. He became more and more excited as he witnessed the magic of the "loaves and the fishes" taking place. Our kitchen table slowly filled with enough of his favorite menu items to provide his daily bread for an entire week.

As Doug transitioned to only soft foods, she made homemade potpies, deviled eggs, banana pudding, and other appetizing foods he could still eat and enjoy.

This same wonderful woman discovered a secret to encourage Doug to eat as he began to resist. While feeding him during their Saturday cooking fests, she began putting a little of her applesauce on the front end of a spoonful of food. Doug would open his mouth as soon as the taste and temperature of cold applesauce touched his lips. In the book of blessings Doug kept, he appropriately expressed his gratitude for his food friend by naming her Saint Janet.

At the end, swallowing liquids became problematic for Doug. I was directed to buy a thickening powder to prevent him from getting aspiration pneumonia. After consideration, I just couldn't bring myself to do that. Instead, I devised a creative way to thicken his liquids while maintaining their taste and pleasure for him. A blender was my secret weapon. For hydration, I made water slushies by blending water and crushed ice. In his coffee, I added vanilla or coffee ice cream to make iced coffees. Cranberry juice was thickened with canned jellied cranberries and apple juice with fresh apples or applesauce. I used chocolate nutritional drinks, such as Boost, Special K, or Ensure, to make shakes. There was no limit to my creative cocktails.

Though at the time I had no idea what the next day would bring, I am forever grateful I made Doug's last dinner special. I was delighted as I watched him enjoy a homemade potpie and a large chocolate shake.

Appropriately, after Doug's memorial service, a packed church flowed into the parish hall for a repast of food and fellowship. Friends provided all of Doug's favorite foods. One of my former students made forty pounds of chicken salad. The faculty from the school I had left two decades before contributed significantly also. What a special send-off, custom-cooked for this special man.

In the words of the familiar African-American folksong, "Let us break bread together, we are one." And we remain one.

DONNA BROWN BENTON

I've Come to Clean Your Shoes

EARLY IN MY career in education, I was teaching a class entitled Living until You Die. Part of the syllabus addressed responding to and supporting others experiencing serious illness, loss, or death. There was no designated textbook for the course, so I was always on the lookout for informational and inspirational readings from various sources. In our home, we had stacks of *Reader's Digest* magazines. Doug's mother automatically renewed his subscription yearly as part of his unrequested birthday gift. One evening, while plopped on the couch and perusing issues that were in arm's reach, I ran across a story with a quirky title that encouraged me to read more. "I've Come to Clean Your Shoes" was originally published in the December 1983 issue.

The story begins with the reader learning about a car crash death in the author's out-of-town family. She is in shock but still attempting to function well enough to ready the family to travel to the funeral. A neighbor friend rings her doorbell and simply states, "I've come to clean your shoes." In a grief fog, she asks him to repeat. He explains he wants to help, and this was his way. Someone had done this for him when his father died, and he is paying it forward. She complied and gathered the family's shoes. He got to work while she continued planning and packing to leave. He left as quietly as he came, leaving all the shined shoes in a line against one wall. He had even scrubbed the soles so the author could put the shoes directly into the suitcases. She summarized, writing, "We left for the airport. Ahead lay grim, sad days, but the image of a quiet man, perhaps a Christ figure, kneeling on my kitchen floor cleaning our shoes, would sustain me."

I decided to use this article for a teachable topic and discussion with my current classes. I was persuaded by this article and hoped my classes, present and future, would be as well. I realized that when I would learn of a sudden tragedy for any of my colleagues, friends, or neighbors, I would send a card expressing my care and support. I would close with the sincere statement, "If I can do anything to help, don't hesitate to let me know." Although well-meaning, the offer stopped short. My thoughts and feelings needed to translate into action.

I assigned the article to my class for reading. I then asked them to write about why it is counterproductive to put the burden of requesting and receiving help on the already-struggling person. During our discussions, the students came to the consensus that when tragedy strikes, people are often in shock or a grief fog. They are diminished and merely trying to survive. Often, people suffering loss are not thinking clearly and might not even know what they need or want. We added that some people of a certain stripe find it hard to ask for help even if they identify a need.

This article delivered on its stated promise: "This powerful story will convince you to stop saying 'Let me know if you need anything.'" That's exactly what it did for me. The author of the article summed up my learnings well. In the closing paragraph, she writes,

> Now whenever I hear of an acquaintance who has lost a loved one, I no longer call with the vague offer, "If there's anything I can do …". Instead, I try to think of one specific task that suits that person's need. And if the person asks, "How did you know I needed that done?" I reply, "It's because a man once cleaned my shoes."

Upon Doug's diagnosis, people who had gone through dementia or a similar illness or sudden tragedy "came to clean our shoes," and though their help and kindness took on different forms, each moved into action:

- A retired social security agent helped us navigate this complicated system and lengthy process to apply for social security disability.
- A lawyer friend in Doug's band worked pro bono with Doug to complete a durable power of attorney, a living will, a medical surrogate, and more.
- A dear friend gifted me a recording device to capture Doug's stories and music. She shared privately with me how she longed for the sound of the voices of her lost loved ones.
- A new teacher who was on the same faculty as I was realized he lived near us. He gave me a pink index card listing his suggestions of how he may be able to help me. I took him up on many of his offers, including taking in my sub plans when Doug's immediate needs caused me to be abruptly absent on a given day.

These and so many more kind actions carried us through. I still remember every giver and every kindness shown to us. These inspirational acts continue to inspire *me* to pay it forward and clean someone else's shoes.

DONNA BROWN BENTON

DONNA BROWN BENTON

It Takes a Village

ALZHEIMER'S AFFECTS THE entire family. All four of us were being affected. Each of us had continual and changing needs. Our individual needs were relentlessly compounding. As the matriarch, I was constantly responding to Doug, as husband and patient, and to our two daughters in their early teens as well. It didn't take long to realize that if we were going to survive, and hopefully thrive during this time, we weren't going to do it alone. We were going to need a lot of help. The proverbial expression "It takes a village" came to mind. Where could we turn? On whom could we count? Who would make up our village? Initially, it was consoling to assume we could count on both Doug's and my extended families. Several long-standing friends came to mind as well.

As we moved forward, we reached out and others reached in. We were grateful to everyone who stepped forward to volunteer and to those who responded when asked. Doug, as the beneficiary, was touched and would quietly add each to his book of blessings.

While Doug was counting our blessings, I was unfortunately starting to struggle with our increased needs and all that we were already asking of our village. Usually, when people offer to help, it's for a limited period of time, such as providing meals for a few weeks while someone recovers from surgery. This was a long-term situation that would go on for years. It was unrealistic to expect people to commit for the duration. While our needs were increasing, I was anticipating our basis of support would be shrinking. I started taking attendance mentally. I realized some of the family and friends we'd put in the "can count on" column never showed up and some had dropped out of Doug's life. I just couldn't believe, or accept, that they had ghosted Doug at the time in his life when he needed them the most. I only hope he wasn't aware of their absence. I chose to suffer in silence and never address this with any of those folks. That might not have been the healthiest approach, but I didn't want to permanently alienate these people and, thereby, compound the loss. Thus, I made the decision to take a rational approach instead of my usual emotional response. My resolve was to eliminate my expectations of the people I thought should respond and to accept the limitations of all people.

I kept my eye on Doug as a role model. He was living in childlike receptivity and delighted in each person who came forward.

I was able to slowly surrender my judgments since I didn't know people's motives. I came to know that some people were tending their own fires just as I was. People can't give what they don't have. Some couldn't bear seeing Doug decline. Some couldn't face the possibility of dementia happening to them. Alzheimer's is the condition most feared by older adults. Others had their own reasons, known only to them.

Instead of focusing on the negative, I decided to highlight the positive. Everyone is a gift. I focused on all the family and friends who made up our village. I was especially delighted by all the surprise people who came through for us in unexpected ways. I became more appreciative, and what you appreciate appreciates. Our village did indeed surround us and enabled us to survive, even thrive. In gratitude and remembering all who were there for us, I am committed to paying it forward and being a part of a village for others in need.

DONNA BROWN BENTON

Counting on Our Community

THIS WAS MY maiden voyage as a caregiver for a loved one diagnosed with dementia. I knew nothing about Alzheimer's. I didn't even know what I didn't know, nor what actions I needed to take and in what order. Luckily, it didn't need to be done all at once or immediately. The needs of a diagnosed person with Alzheimer's are fluid; old needs change, and new needs surface as the disease progresses.

In addition to our strong personal support network of family and friends, it became obvious we needed access to professional support and services from our local community.

Doug was past the point of being able to accomplish this task, so I sprang into action. This was second nature for me. My extroverted self has always been skilled at sourcing services, networking, and making connections. So now, whatever the current crisis or newly surfaced need, I'd ask everyone I knew: friends, neighbors, work colleagues, church members, and total strangers. I also searched newspapers, local magazines, newsletters, and church bulletins. I listened to the radio and television, made calls, and searched online. I consulted referral services and agencies. I may have missed some opportunities, but I was amazed by the community connections and resources available to us. Also amazing was how both Doug and I benefited from all that was bestowed on him.

Of course, the Alzheimer's Association was my first call. I registered Doug for their Safe Return Program created to enhance the national response to wandering Alzheimer's patients. This program ensures the safe return of these individuals to caregivers by assisting in the identification of lost memory-impaired people. Doug willingly wore his ID-numbered necklace. Thankfully, Doug never got lost, but the program served to reassure me of his protection throughout. We wanted to support the Alzheimer's Association's funding for research, so a fellow teacher organized a group to join her family and Doug and me at the annual Walk to End Alzheimer's the first fall after Doug's diagnosis. We were also blessed to attend their candlelight vigil for those living with Alzheimer's and in memory of those who have died from the disease.

A housing agency timely offered small grants to individual homeowners to make an improvement that would enable the disabled person to continue living in their own home. Knowing wandering would be an obstacle to keeping Doug at home, I completed the simple grant process, applying to erect a fence around our yard. Our request was accepted, and we were able to have the fence built. What a gift it proved to be as it enabled Doug to safely remain in our home as designed.

The community at Presentation Academy, a local Catholic high school, enveloped our youngest daughter and significantly shaped the woman she is today. She had chosen to attend "Pres" with her friends. But sadly, between application and registration, her father declined and had to leave his employment. That meant there was no money available for tuition costs. Our daughter, already struggling with her father's diagnosis, now had to accept this compounded loss. When we didn't attend registration as scheduled, the principal called to inquire. I explained our current situation. The amazing principal invited Doug, me, and our daughter, to meet with her at the school to seek a solution. When we arrived, the principal had already secured a scholarship from a generous benefactor and gifted our daughter with all her textbooks as well. We still refer to this as our miracle on South Fourth Street.

When Doug was no longer ambulatory, he required additional services. Veterans Medical Center had a special wheelchair assembled to accommodate his six-foot-six height. After Doug's use of it was satisfied, I contacted the Kentucky Office of Vocational Rehab to donate Doug's chair. By doing so, I was able to pay forward the great gift Doug was given. Serendipitously, that same week, the outreach coordinator received a call from a family in desperate need of a wheelchair for a person of Doug's height. WDRB television station ran the story during their local newscast. As a direct result of one gift given and then shared, this agency, in turn, received endless calls from folks offering wheelchairs they no longer needed to benefit others.

When Doug eventually became homebound, two other unmet needs arose. These may sound small but were large in importance. One was Doug's hair care. He had always attended to his appearance and was well-groomed. The hairstylist who had cut his hair for years generously offered to come to our home to continue taking care of him. She'd bring her special equipment to shampoo his hair while he was sitting in his wheelchair or lying in bed. She would then cut and blow-dry his hair as well. He'd always smile when she arrived and throughout the process. What a tremendous service to Doug. It made me realize what an unmet need this must be for other homebound folks. Our experience was not a one-off. I recently spoke to a woman who shared that her husband's longtime barber also comes to their home to continue serving and to stay connected to his client-turned-friend, who is also homebound with Alzheimer's.

I never imagined a dentist could, or would, make house calls, but I happily learned of at least two in our city who do. Continuing good oral hygiene for Doug became a challenge due to the loss of his ability to navigate to our bathroom sink and the functional skills needed to perform these tasks. Infections were occurring with some regularity, and Doug was risking sepsis. Hospice recommended a dentist who came as needed and was tremendously helpful professionally. He was also kind and caring to Doug. As fate would have it, the dentist was scheduled to come the morning Doug slipped into a coma. I called to cancel. Their response was above and beyond. He and his office staff sent a sympathy card expressing care and support.

Again, this dentist was not a one-off. I know a nursing home patient who lost her dentures. The home arranged for their van to take her in her wheelchair to the parking lot at the dentist's office. The dentist and his assistant came into the van to take the necessary dental impressions. I was privileged to witness his presence and professionalism. I teared up watching how kindly he worked with her. What wonderful hidden heroes!

The Archdiocese of Louisville offered two unique experiences that provided us with spiritual support. Doug was blessed to attend a Gennesaret retreat for the seriously ill. The retreat staff was led by a priest who attended to the spiritual health of the retreatants as well as a medical team who holistically cared for the participants. Doug was so blessed by attending the retreat. He played guitar for mass and received the sacrament of the sick.

The other unique gift from archdiocesan priest Father Ron Knott came the first Christmas after Doug died in September. My daughters and I had been dreading the first Christmas without him. We considered avoiding mass, as we knew everyone else would be celebratory and singing "Joy to the World." A neighbor shared that a Blue Christmas Mass was available only for those grieving. What a perfect Christmas gift for us. We attended and relished the soft music, an appropriately themed homily, and shared fellowship with others who were also experiencing a blue Christmas.

I'm so indebted to each of the community connections who served Doug and cared for him. Their services enabled him to have the best quality of life for the longest possible time. May these community connections continue to flourish, and may others rise up. May each person living with dementia receive the care they need from their local community connections.

DONNA BROWN BENTON

My Life Flows on in Endless Song

D OUG WAS A musician. He was most alive when he was making music. He was innately gifted. In high school, he played saxophone with the marching band and, as the top student, was chosen to receive the John Philip Sousa Band Award for superior musicianship and outstanding dedication. He also brought his musical talents to the school's thespian productions. He was perfectly cast as Conrad Birdie in *Bye Bye Birdie,* singing and playing his electric guitar.

Early in his teenage years, Doug was drafted to fill in for the bass guitarist in a working band. Subbing paved the way for a permanent path of playing rock and roll over four decades. Doug insisted he would not still be playing "Proud Mary" at the age of forty. He was. On his fortieth birthday, I took a decorated cake to his band job. The tombstone on the cake read, "Rest in Peace, Proud Mary."

Doug's life of playing and singing spans both the secular and the sacred. On Saturday nights, he was an electric bassist on stage and, on Sunday mornings, a minister of music in the sanctuary. Luckily, he never mixed up his playlists. It was hard not to focus on this tall, dark, and handsome guitar player in front of the congregation. A close friend once teased me as we walked together to the church service. "Do you remember when you used to go to church to pray instead of to watch the guitar player play?"

Doug knew the way to my heart was through his music. While dating, he wrote songs for me that still cause me to swoon. He composed a song and sang for our nuptial mass, and at our wedding reception, he performed with his band. Doug also played and sang at our daughters' baptisms. Through our thirty-four years, we attended every James Taylor and Eagles concert within driving distance. Our family took Doug in a wheelchair to the Eagles concert at the KFC Yum Center in Louisville. That event marked the first concert at the Yum Center and the last concert Doug was able to attend. What a bittersweet, emotional evening. Doug bought and constantly played every LP, then cassette, then CD ever made by his favorite artists, including James Taylor, the Beatles, and the Eagles. For the first three-quarters of Doug's life, he successfully and continuously played and sang in performing bands.

Sadly, during the last quarter of his life, Alzheimer's put Doug on a losing streak. While still in the early stage, he had to make the difficult decision to leave the band he loved and was a vital part of for years. Doug went to practice on Wednesday nights, and by the time he got to the band jobs on the weekends, he couldn't remember new arrangements they'd rehearsed. Doug was such a perfectionist about his music that he couldn't continue in good conscience. I can only speculate on the magnitude of that indescribable loss.

Through the years, the losses continued in his musical life. One of the most poignant moments for me was when Doug asked me for my help. Between his thumb and forefinger, he clutched one of his Fender guitar picks. Looking bewildered, he said, "I can't quite remember what this is."

> Through all the tumult and the strife, I hear that music ringing. It finds an echo in my soul.
> How can I keep from singing?
>
> (Christian Hymn by Pauline T. and Robert Lowry)

Despite the professional and personal losses of performing, Doug continued his relationship with music. He did keep singing, and at home, for a time, continued to play both his electric and acoustic guitars. Our daughter downloaded all his favorite music onto iPods that he listened to and enjoyed nonstop. His band's drummer gave us a DVD of a benefit concert their band performed. We played that DVD for Doug repeatedly for years. He never tired of watching it and responding. (I picked up where Doug left off and still watch it regularly.) Through the progression of Doug's decline, it was amazing to watch the role music still played. Despite losing recall of most words to speak, Doug continued to know the lyrics to songs. Then, when he was unable to speak, he continued to mouth the words. Everyone who witnessed it was awestruck as he continued to tap in perfect time, airplay his guitar, and respond to any form of musical stimulus. We used Doug's retained familiarity with numerous songs as a vehicle of communication. For example, we sang, "Sit down, sit down, you're rocking the boat" from *Guys and Dolls* as an entertaining and effective way to get him to sit down. When words failed, music continued to speak.

We benefited from the positive studies and research centered on Alzheimer's and music, but we didn't need them to convince us. We witnessed and experienced with Doug what all the findings showed. Music was his best medicine. His informal music therapy was an adjunct treatment as powerful as all the pharmaceutical drugs he was swallowing. Music was a mood elevator and served as a calming influence when needed. The ability of music to conjure up vivid memories is a phenomenon well known to brain researchers. Familiar and likable music can reduce depression and lessen agitation. We saw Doug's rock and roll reconnect him to his treasured past and allow him to, in the words of Bob Seger, "reminisce about the days of old." Music

DONNA BROWN BENTON

improved the quality of Doug's life and our shared life with him. It served as a great source of socialization, as fellow musicians came often to make music for Doug.

I heard Jon Batiste share his belief that "music is a spiritual radar that finds the person when they need it most." Music continued to find Doug in his need. As the Seger song continues, "Still like that old-time rock and roll, that kind of music just soothes the soul." Music was safe in his soul. It continued to be his constant companion to the very end. Music was his lifeline.

In response to Doug's online obituary, two of Doug's fellow musicians each posted touching tributes.

> I can't remember if I cried when I read about his widowed bride.
> But something touched me deep inside, the day the music died.
> ("American Pie" by Don McLean)

And the other:

> I look at you all, see the love there that's sleeping, while my guitar gently weeps. I look at the world and I notice it's turning, still my guitar gently weeps.
> ("While My Guitar Gently Weeps" by the Beatles)

The highlight of Doug's memorial mass was, appropriately, the music. The music ministry was powerful and a fitting tribute to Doug's life and love of music.

In sympathy and support, and in lieu of flowers, many sent wind chimes with such sentiments as "May the sounds be a gentle reminder of the music Doug brought to our lives." I strategically placed each chime surrounding our home and in Doug's memorial garden. In addition to the wind, our grandchildren delight in making them ring harmoniously.

In the November after Doug's death, we attended the annual hospice memorial service, remembering and honoring patients who had died the preceding year. Each year, Hosparus Health chooses a different theme for the focus. Our family experienced Doug's presence when we arrived and discovered that the theme for that year was music. The program design, readings, reflections, and music were all centered on remembering your loved ones through music. The mementos we received read, "In the sweetness of song, I remember you." How true.

The three-part inscription we chose for Doug's cremains internment sculpture ends with "Doug, your music plays on." It does.

The first and last verse

1981 marked our first Valentine's Day married. There was excitement, heart fluttering and hopeful expectations. My musician husband secretly hired his cousin's quartet from Pride of Kentucky Chorus to serenade me with love songs during my marriage class at Assumption. All the women in the room were wowed! Slowly over the next three decades, our romantic love evolved into unconditional love. As Valentine's Day 2013 approached, my heart painfully knew this may be our last. Since Alzheimer's had taken everything from Doug but his music, the inspiration came to me to close the circle. This time I hired the same quartet to come to our home and serenade him with our love songs. We gathered around his wheelchair and began to sing. Amazingly and miraculously, he attempted to mouth the words and harmonize. He held my hand and smiled with deep knowing and loving. All the women in the room cried in harmony. Doug, your love lives on, your music plays on.
- **Donna Benton, Louisville**

ILLUMINATING THE ALZHEIMER'S PATH

Hosparus Health provided an additional blessing when I discovered that a former teaching colleague played the harp for patients at their palliative care center. When Fran learned of Doug's Hosparus Health enrollment, she graced our home weekly and soothed our souls and spirits with her presence and her harp music. Doug

DONNA BROWN BENTON

and I would sing along as she played "You Are My Sunshine." Both he and I teared up when we'd get to the plea, "Please don't take my sunshine away." The harpist closed each harmonious session with this lullaby:

> Like a light in the darkness, I'll hold you awhile.
> We'll rock on the water, I'll cradle you deep
> And I'll hold you while angels sing you to sleep.

(Chris Williamson)

When Doug slipped into a coma, Fran came to his bedside and brought her full-sized harp, as she had promised Doug she would sometime. This time, I cradled Doug deep while angels sang him to sleep. Fran closed their musical circle by playing at Doug's memorial service. At each visit, Fran played and sang about angels and served as one for Doug and me. It is no wonder that heavenly angels are often portrayed as playing harps.

Doug and I shared a deep musical kinship with another married couple, Donna and Wes, former teaching colleagues of mine. For years, they hosted us for special musical events at their home. They were each gifted musicians and were adept at playing many varied instruments. When Doug could no longer travel to their home, the couple packed up their instruments and made their way to our home numerous times. Each session was a blessing and the best form of ministry for a soulful musician like Doug.

Our musician friends also played and sang for the dedication of Doug's memorial garden and his first anniversary of death commemoration. It was cloudy when we began the service in the memory garden. Just

DONNA BROWN BENTON

as they started playing and singing the Beatles song "Here Comes the Sun," the sun came out from behind the clouds and shone on cue. Receiving that as a sign of Doug's presence brightened our day. The music of Wes and Donna also plays on.

DONNA BROWN BENTON

Seeking Spiritual Sundays

DOUG AND I met in a Catholic lay community that each of us independently joined as spiritual seekers. Our shared spiritual values played a large role in our initial attraction to each other and, ultimately, in our marriage commitment. We became soulmates who supported each other's spiritual growth. Marrying Catholic, our vows included the promise to raise any children to love God and God's church. As a family, we were vitally involved in creating and participating in the life of our parish church.

This enduring pattern and spiritual practice of church participation came to a slow, then abrupt, halt. The Sunday came when Doug no longer could perform his music ministry duties and serve as a lector for the Word of God. More prohibitive for church attendance were his mobility issues. Suddenly, Sunday morning was foreign to us.

Initially, I secretly enjoyed staying home instead of attending church services. By Sunday morning, I was relieved not to have to don my professional attire and instead could stay in my pajamas. No more alarm clock. We initiated what we called "natural rise." Together, we consumed caffeine, read the Sunday newspaper, and watched *CBS Sunday Morning*. We teased that, like other lax churchgoers, we now temporarily attended "Saint Mattress of the Springs." As the Lionel Richie song recounts, it was "easy like Sunday morning."

Eventually, the novelty and enjoyment of our newfound Sunday morning freedom began to fade. It took me a while to miss what had been integral my whole life. I was getting in touch with my longings. All the ways I had traditionally tapped into in order to grow spiritually were not available to me. I had to take a leave of absence from our spiritual sharing book group. I wasn't free to attend mindfulness classes. And, of course, I missed worshiping with our church community, the rituals, music, readings, and homilies that spoke to me. I was cut off and withering instead of growing spiritually.

During this spiritual plateau, two friends with whom we'd bonded while we were all members of the same church community came to visit. I shared our spiritual vacuum and asked how they were filling the void. They had discovered Oprah's *Super Soul Sunday*. They were persuasive and convinced us to tune in as well. I grilled them about the particulars regarding time and network so we wouldn't miss out.

When we tuned in for the first time, we were greeted with Oprah's standard introduction that I came to know by heart. "I wanted a place where people could go every Sunday to wake up, thought-provoking, eye-opening. This will lift you right up. It's food for your soul every single Sunday." That was exactly what we were looking for. Oprah's vision matched our need—a match made in heaven. This spiritual practice found us. Who could have imagined such a blessing would come via television? The secular and the sacred merged.

Each Sunday morning, Doug and I sat together in our home sanctuary with candles lit. Each hour-long segment featured Oprah dialoging with various spiritual teachers, preachers, and authors, such as Mitch Albom of *Tuesdays with Morrie*. Some guests shared their story that provided a message and meaning applicable to our own lives. Each was different, yet all shared a common thread of spiritual, psychological, and relational growth. Topics such as faith, forgiveness, gratitude, and grief were all included. Many evoked emotions, and Doug and I would be moved to tears. Over time, I'm not certain how much Doug was able to process or retain but this practice remained a shared spiritual experience and energy between us.

I took notes for retention and integration into my life. We watched for years—often, there were shows we had already seen. I never labeled them "repeats." They served as a renewal or refresher to hear again. I had takeaways from each session.

I so often talked about and quoted *Super Soul Sunday* that all our family and friends knew it had become our hybrid church. Without our asking, they waited until Sunday afternoon to call or come by.

I was amazed at how I grew spiritually by such unconventional means. The universe provides, sometimes in the most unexpected ways. It filled a void and was the sustenance we needed to continue moving forward on our Alzheimer's pilgrimage. Indeed, each Sunday proved to be super for our souls.

You are covered
in prayer

This Prayer Blanket has
been prayed over and
blessed by a priest of
St. Brigid St. James
Community

DONNA BROWN BENTON

Blanketed and Comforted

A HEARTWARMING STORY FROM my early childhood that my mother often recounted was the relationship between my blue blanket and me. I creatively called her "my blue" and was clearly attached and devoted to her. My mom struggled to pry her away from me long enough to launder her every Monday, washday. Since this was long before clothes dryers, Mom hung everything with clothespins on our backyard clothesline. As the story goes, blankie and I were so bonded that I would stand under the damp blanket cuddling the corner while sucking my thumb until the blanket was dry and back in my arms.

Both of our daughters inherited my blanket gene. Based on my washday separation anxiety, I had the foresight to buy each daughter two of the same blankets. Julia's was yellow and named Dewey. Erica's was aqua and named No-No. Don't ask me about the origins of either of the names of their blankets. The blankets were so loved and used for comfort that I mended the worn spots and replaced the binding continually throughout their childhoods.

In hospital birthing rooms, many of us were swaddled in pink and blue baby blankets, photographed, and presented to our parents. Later, as parents ourselves, we in turn swaddled our infants for warmth and to mimic the secure quarters of the womb.

Over the years, I've observed that security blankets aren't only for babies and children. Adults are using them and giving them to fulfill many of the same purposes. When hospitalized for any procedures, I'm begging my nurses to cover me with an endless supply of heated blankets. I've often observed groups offering prayer or support blankets to those whom they want to wrap in prayer and care at times of illness or suffering.

During COVID-19, I was invited to be part of such an initiative. My nephew's wife was undergoing chemo and radiation for cancer treatment. With her compromised immune system, many of us could not be physically present. Her close friends reached out. We were asked to trace our hands onto a fabric square. They were then pieced into a large quilt. Each of us was seen as symbolically reaching out to and holding her. That experience enabled me to be in a position of giving. Later, I was a recipient. When a dear girlfriend died too young, I was given two of her treasured, oversized scarves, big enough to function as wraps. They were handmade, beautifully designed batiks in regal colors of purples, greens, and golds. I feel so connected to my friend when I wear them as a scarf statement as she often had. When I'm missing her and want to experience a hug from her, I wrap myself in one of her scarves.

Based upon all these blanket experiences, I started brainstorming what I could create for Doug to serve the same purposes. Doug was a big T-shirt wearer, so that was the source of my inspiration. As soon as he got home from work daily, he quickly shed his suit and changed into one of his numerous T-shirts. We bought him a T-shirt at every concert we attended and brought home a T-shirt souvenir from each trip. We also secured "Dad shirts" from our daughters' high schools and colleges, *MASH* and Doug's favorite TV shows, *Forrest Gump* and Doug's other favorite movies, his bands, and so many more sources. I had his T-shirts made into a personal quilt, the fleece backing providing warmth and comfort. The quilt served the dual purpose of security and as a visual life review, reminders of his favorite things. I believe that the quilt was a boost to help him reconnect to his fading life experiences and memories. The quilt lives on as I now wrap up in it often and fondly.

Doug's other blanket gift was from our parish. St. James was our daughters' school community and our family's faith community for two decades. During his dementia journey, the parish gifted Doug with a prayer blanket made by the parishioners and blessed by our priest. On the blanket was a pocket that contained a prayer card that promised, "You are covered in prayer." This lap quilt softly covered him while he sat in his wheelchair or nested in his favorite living room chair. He would clasp it and hold it close.

Several years separated Doug from participating in parish life. Being absent from his faith community was another loss Doug faced. When we returned for Doug's memorial mass, it was supportive to be surrounded by and reconnected with so many of our faithful friends in our faith community. The prayer blanket helped bridge that gap in a symbolic yet real way.

DONNA BROWN BENTON

One Disease, Two Perspectives

SYMPATHY ENTAILS FEELINGS of pity and sorrow for someone else's misfortune. Empathy is the ability to understand and share the feelings of another, to be able to walk a mile in someone else's shoes. I definitely wanted to empathize with Doug, but I wondered if I was able to since I had zero prior experience living with dementia. Could I shift from my caregiving, spousal view and expand to include and prioritize Doug's perspective as the patient?

With this daunting challenge in mind, I received an insight from Doug's doctor. I privately shared with him that I was going crazy because my husband couldn't let me out of his sight. He was on my heels in and out of every room. He shadowed me all day, every day. The doctor smiled and nodded knowingly. "Did you ever play peekaboo with your daughters?" he asked.

"Endlessly," I responded.

"For babies, that game works because in their early cognition, if an object can't be seen, it no longer exists—object permanence. By playing, you were teaching your daughters that even if you couldn't be seen, you continued to exist. Do you also remember their laughter and excitement when you would reappear?" the doctor continued. "Doug's condition will no longer allow him to relearn that principle or apply it. For him, if he can't see you, he can't conceptualize that you are present." My heart broke for Doug as I realized the childlike panic he must have felt when I was no longer in his sight. My annoyance instantly turned to acceptance.

I also received help adjusting to Doug's perspective on two different but similar experiences that happened a week apart. We were trying to decide if it was feasible to fly separately using airline vouchers that were about to expire. It would require Doug and our two teenaged daughters to fly together. I would need to fly separately and reunite with them at our final destination. From my perspective, besides the obvious fiscal savings, I was confident Doug would be safe due to our daughters' maturity and airport personnel support.

Last night we were trying to decide whether to fly seperatly to Florida to visit Jamie or to fly together which meant losing $$ on previously purchased tickets. The plan was for Julia, Erica & I to fly out Friday & Donna Saturday. I became "panic stricken" at the thought of navigating through airports & flight changes (like Atlanta) with just myself to find the way. Donna helped me to see that Julia & Erica could help me but if I didn't feel comfortable - she would change her ticket. This made me feel like a child because of my anxiety, but at least we could still talk about it. Eventually, we came to an agreement that I would be OK (there are personell to help you @ the airport as well as my daughters. So, we didn't lose any money (not that this was a big issue with Donna; she's more concerned for my feelings). So, we're going the first week of April.

Doug's journal captured his very different perspective.

DONNA BROWN BENTON

A week later, Doug was battling insecurity and getting lost driving. One Friday night, Doug had dropped off our daughter at a friend's house on the other side of town. I never anticipated his inability to pick her up there just hours later.

> Had "directions" to pick up
> Erica at a new freind's house in the
> East End. Got to the "subdivision"
> and couldn't find any of the streets.
> Finally went to a pay phone, called Donna
> & she called the house where Erica was &
> they brought her to me. It was HUMILIATING.
> Visibility was very poor, but I still kicked
> myself. This happened once before in the
> same general area when we had a New Year's Dance
> to play for in the same general area.
> I used to be "Mr Directions". Now that
> this is going downhill too... I'm wondering if
> I should consider not driving. I become
> confused and am upset with myself which only
> make the situation worse! I'm pretty depressed
> now about it. I think I'll let it settle for
> a few days.

Doug's distress about getting lost is captured in this journal entry.

One of the most poignant moments calling for my empathetic response still pierces my heart. Obviously, up to this point, Doug had dressed himself for more than five decades. One day, he shuffled and waddled into the kitchen and stood before me, arms outstretched, completely confused and perplexed. He had his tight, straight-leg jeans on backward. He must have known something was wrong because he couldn't walk well but had no idea how to remedy the situation. It was a long walk as I slowly ushered him back to our room. I could only imagine the depth of what this independent, well-dressed, exacting man must be experiencing. Not wanting to add to his distress, I resorted to a little sincere humor. "Doug, I always enjoy undressing you, so now it's going to be my pleasure to dress you as well." He smiled.

I always strove to be empathetic with Doug. Sometimes I was only sympathetic; sometimes I was neither. I forgave myself for the times I couldn't or didn't see Doug's perspective through his eyes. I remembered and rejoiced in the times I did. Most importantly, I treasured Doug's ongoing, unconditional love for me and my ongoing, unconditional love for him. About that, we always shared the same perspective.

Life is not measured
by the number of breaths
we take,
but by the moments
that take our breath away.

DONNA BROWN BENTON

Silver Anniversary, Golden Moments

DOUG AND I were sentimental and loved to commemorate and celebrate all the large and small relationship milestones: our first date, our engagement on June 21, and all our wedding anniversaries on December 20. During the first year of our marriage, we celebrated each month on the twentieth, then annually, with years like the first, fifth, tenth, and fifteenth receiving special emphasis.

Though our wedding anniversaries were full of romance, we also intentionally kept it real. We would each make or select and write a card that reflected our past year and our hopes for the coming year.

through thinness and through thickness,
in joy and in home improvement...

This card addresses the realness of relationships that most anniversary cards gloss over. Part of me was depressed as our anniversary was approaching because I felt like we didn't have much to celebrate this year. What came to me today was to celebrate the faithfulness & commitment even though it has been hard and to celebrate the hope of what our future together can hold. →

I uncovered this card written on our eleventh wedding anniversary.

By our eighteenth anniversary, Doug had been diagnosed. Each year, despite my attempts not to, I wondered if this would be our last anniversary. I hoped the progression of his symptoms saved him from the same thoughts. We never spoke about it aloud, each of us trying to spare the other.

At the time of Doug's diagnosis, we were told the average lifespan for early-onset was eight years. We were at seven years and fading. It was evident we weren't going to reach our golden wedding anniversary as we had hoped. Longevity of married love and fidelity is a noble calling we had hoped to achieve.

I decided to move our golden anniversary celebration forward twenty-five years and began to plan a full gala acknowledging our silver wedding anniversary. Our friends and family all rallied to make it possible. We sent formal invitations and started praying that when the day came, Doug would still be present, literally and figuratively.

We creatively decorated and transformed a church hall for a sit-down dinner and dance reception. Our chef friends prepared, and everyone enjoyed, a five-star meal. After cutting the Italian cream cake, it was time for dancing. A fellow teacher friend offered to DJ for us, playing all the songs Doug and I enjoyed throughout our relationship. For hours, everyone did the hustle, YMCA, and twist and slow danced. The DJ then invited everyone to encircle us as we reenacted our first dance from our wedding. Our chosen song was a waltz to Anne Murray's "Can I Have This Dance?" At our wedding reception, we wowed everyone by dancing a waltz, but those dance skills were in the past. That night, we just wrapped our arms around each other and swayed to the music. Since Doug was fourteen inches taller than I was, I was always looking up to him, and our eyes were locked. To everyone's amazement, Doug broke his Alzheimer's-induced intermittent silence, recalled the words, and began to sing to me again.

> Can I have this dance for the rest of my life?
> Will you be my partner every night?
> When we're together, it feels so right.
> Can I have this dance for the rest of my life?

There was a collective audible gasp and then silence as everyone realized what they were witnessing. What a golden, last-forever moment.

Despite our original dreams, we didn't make it to fifty years of marriage. I came to accept that there was nothing magical about the number fifty. Our love and fidelity were strong, if not long. Doug's spirit was willing, but his flesh was weak. What a double blessing if a couple gets quality and quantity in a relationship. We did not have a golden wedding anniversary but did have thirty-four golden years of marriage made of many golden moments and memories.

DONNA BROWN BENTON

DONNA BROWN BENTON

Regrets, I've Had a Few

A S FAR BACK as I remember, I've loved songs and will listen to them over and over. The repetition was so consistent that I came to know the words easily, without working to memorize them. The focus of songs for me was always the words, lyrics, verses, and refrains. While singing with or listening to them, I'd spend a lot of time reflecting on the meaning, the message of each song. I'd try to imagine what life experiences occurred for the writer that resulted in this particular song. I'd think about whether I agreed or disagreed with the takeaway to be inferred. I'd be moved by the emotions expressed. I'd allow some of the songs to find a home in me and influence my behavior.

When we met and married, Doug and I happily discovered our common love for songs and so many of the same musicians. As with everything else, we came at music from very different perspectives but were still able to find harmony. For Doug, it was all about the precision of the instrumentation, playing, singing, and performing.

We both sang, shared, and loved Frank Sinatra's "My Way." For the first half of my life, this song gave me permission to be OK with whom I was then discovering myself to be. I was independent and strong-willed. I was not as conforming as the authority figures in my life would have preferred. Instead, I wanted to see and do things my way.

In the same song, I was empowered by the treatment of regrets. Retrospectively, Sinatra sings of living a life that was full. There are references to tasting it all, biting off more than one could chew, and eating it up. Then when the end is near and he's ready to take "that final curtain," he has only a few regrets. As I envisioned my life, I also wanted to live it fully with few regrets. This song was an inspiration. I could do this. I set that intention and charted the course for myself for "each careful step along the byway …."

The second half of my life taught me the deeper lesson of the song about regrets. I realized it wasn't only about my having few regrets from my life. Perhaps even more significantly, it's about living relationally with few regrets affecting the quality of every relationship. This insight stayed with me and continued to influence my daily actions and choices, always with the goal of few regrets.

The issue of regrets surfaced intensely for all of us who loved Doug during his illness. As the saying goes, grief and regret don't mix. Doug's dad was deceased, and his mother was an octogenarian. She was naturally grief-stricken about her son's progressive disease. Doug and his mom shared an unbroken bond for five decades. Like many parents of her generation, good parenting meant providing for their son's physical needs in a stable home. Their love was assumed—shown but not spoken or expressed. I am certain she never expected her son to precede her in death. One always thinks you have enough time.

> Dear Doug –
>
> I well remember the day you were born 64 years ago. It was Palm Sunday – a beautiful spring day just for you – and a happy day for us.
>
> Over the years it has somehow been difficult for me to let you know how I was feeling, and how dear you were (and are) to me. But I hope you knew how much I loved you – during the difficult times as well as the happy ones.
>
> I only hope I'm not too late – and that you can somehow sense my love for you – even if you can't understand what I've written
>
> For I love you, my son
> Always have – always will –
> Mom

Since she lived out of town a few hours from us, on what proved to be Doug's second to last birthday, the above touching handwritten letter arrived in the mail from his mother.

DONNA BROWN BENTON

This letter broke my heart for both Doug and his mom, but what a gift for both of them. I continued to read her letter aloud to Doug over and over. He listened intently but was past the point of verbal response. I can only trust that, on some level of consciousness, he received her love. I also trust that the act of her sharing helped heal her regrets, allowed her to express love for her son, and brought her peace.

For me, small regrets showed up after Doug's death. I was shocked by their appearance. I honestly felt I had done everything humanly possible to care for Doug for the duration. Still, "wouldas" and "shouldas" popped up. I was haunted by regrets, such as wishing I had figured out a way to buy a van that could have transported Doug when he was confined to his wheelchair. I hated that he was homebound those last few years. I was tormented by such thoughts, even though I knew they weren't logical and had no foundation. These ideas made me return to the counselor who worked with me throughout.

He assured me this was a very normal part of one's grief journey. I wasn't experiencing true regrets. What I was feeling wasn't rooted in reality. He further explained that because, after your loved one's death, you no longer have the opportunity to do anything else to directly impact your person's life ever again, you start irrationally wishing you had done more while they were alive. He encouraged me instead to focus on what I had done for Doug during the whole of our relationship. Gradually, I was able to reflect on our entire journey together. I am peaceful. Occasionally, I hear Sinatra's song playing and I sing along. "Regrets I've had a few, but then again, too few to mention."

"I miss me too"

DONNA BROWN BENTON

Four Forever Words

I ONCE HEARD AN anecdotal story about Estée Lauder while she was in the midst of Alzheimer's. This story had a profound influence and impact on me.

Estée's son Leonard was interviewed by CBS on the topic of the family business. Leonard was asked, "How hard was it, as a son, to watch your mother, who had been so vibrant, start to deteriorate like that?"

> "It was very hard," he responded. But to her son's credit, instead of lamenting about what he'd been asked about regarding his feelings, he shifted the focus to his mother. He continued, "I remember being with her, and my wife Evelyn came into the room and said, 'Estée, we miss you in the office.' She looked at Evelyn and said, 'I miss me too.'"

I was startled upon learning of Estée's response, and I assume her son and daughter-in-law were as well. This powerful four-word statement made its way into a family business interview. The power of those four spoken words is that they are a rare, first-person account of Alzheimer's. "I miss me too." Most statements about Alzheimer's are second-person voices—you or your—or third-person voices—she, her, he, him, they. How insightful to hear Estée's first-person voice instead of our voice—how Alzheimer's is affecting us, not them.

I recall one of Doug's doctors instructing me that it is incredibly painful for Alzheimer's patients when they are aware of their current condition, when they still know what they don't know and what they are losing. Eventually during the process, they are no longer aware of what they don't know and what they have lost.

I never heard Doug express Estée's summative statement, "I miss me." Without verbalizing those exact words, I know for certain that Doug missed the person he formally identified as. I know he missed the person he once knew himself able to be and able to do. I poignantly remember his expressing the pain of each loss, how he viewed himself in the midst of his disease, and what he formerly enjoyed doing and could no longer do. A few of many examples included being an avid reader, using the computer for work and leisure, playing his bass in his band and his guitar in church, and driving and finding his way anywhere as "Mr. Directions." He spoke of his "former self" and all the medicine he had to take in an attempt to maintain that self.

Estée Lauder's statement left an indelible mark on me. My takeaway is a resolve to focus on the one experiencing incredible, ongoing loss of self and not to focus on myself and my loss in the situation. In addition, I'm determined to encourage those struggling with Alzheimer's to share their stories, to give voice, as able, to what they are experiencing. For my part, I commit to receive what each person shares no matter how difficult it is to hear.

"I miss me too." I hope these four words stay with me forever.

DONNA BROWN BENTON

Continue Communicating

FROM THE BEGINNING, communicating was the hallmark of Doug's and my relationship. While dating, many a night we would talk on the phone until morning. We'd finally hang up when it was time to go to work. Throughout our relationship, we continued to grow and deepen our relationship through open, honest, and sometimes nonverbal communication. When dementia symptoms surfaced, I was committed to ensuring we would communicate to the end.

Even though Doug had dementia, he had the same human needs to be seen and heard, to be acknowledged and accompanied, to be included, and to continue communicating. His desire for connection was stronger than his cognition. He was still able to communicate but not in the same ways.

Shared music and songs continued to be woven into the daily beat of our life together. Music is a language for us. When words fail, music continues to speak. Leonard Bernstein says, "Music can name the unnameable and communicate the unknowable." Thus, we could continue communicating.

Early on in the first stage of his dementia, there were communication changes. Doug repeated stories, was frustrated trying to find the word he wanted, and would lose his train of thought. I would listen to the repeated story each time like it was the first time I'd heard it. I helped him find the word, if he wanted me to, or waited as long as it took for him to find it. I cued him as to where he'd lost his train of thought. I strove to let him know I was patient and listening to him so we could continue communicating.

When Doug could no longer follow my convoluted conversations, I kept it simple and direct, one thought at a time. This enabled Doug to receive the content and process it so we could continue communicating.

In mid-stage, Doug would inject into conversations a random, disconnected, and seemingly rehearsed thought or sentence as a way of being included and still belonging. I, or someone in the group, would respond and build the ensuing conversation on Doug's contribution so we could continue communicating.

When Doug spoke less and withdrew more, others and I acknowledged his presence, called him by name, and spoke to him in a manner that required no response so we could continue communicating.

In the early-end stage, when Doug stopped speaking, which is common for frontotemporal dementia, he could still listen. I continued to talk to him as if nothing had changed. I remember the day our deed of release from our thirty-year home mortgage arrived in the mail. I wanted him to know, because we worked so hard together for decades to pay it down. I told him the whole story, we celebrated, and he smiled with a knowing nod. We could continue communicating.

Without words, we found ways to communicate effectively through touch and our body language, daring to just sit together holding hands, holding each other. Through signs of affection and our own private love language, we could continue to communicate.

When Doug spent the last five days of his life in a coma, our daughters and I continued to speak to him. We could continue communicating our undying love, our support for him, and our presence with him.

In the beginning stages of his dementia, I said I was committed to maintaining constant communication with Doug to the end. In retrospect, I modified my statement of intention. Robert Lowell says, "In the end, there is no end." That has been my lived experience with Doug—there is no end. Doug and I continue communicating. I still talk to him, know his presence, and recognize his responses or reactions. He visits regularly in my dreams. I still find meaning and messages through the songs we shared and those that spoke to us in our relationship. I saved and reread our engagement and marriage encounter journals, all the love letters he wrote, and cards shared for special occasions. Since love never dies, the written expressions of his love are still alive and continue to speak to me. I experience what I refer to as *sacred synchronicity* or *signs* from him. We always have been and always will be united on a soul level. We continue communicating.

DONNA BROWN BENTON

DONNA BROWN BENTON

Life Cycle

IN AN EARLY dementia prognosis appointment, one of Doug's doctors shared a possible prediction, depending on the length of his remaining life span. Dementia patients can be observed to lose their major motor skills in the reverse order that they developed them. Some examples of these milestones are rolling over, sitting by oneself, pulling up to a standing position, taking just a few steps and then walking without holding on, climbing, dressing oneself, feeding oneself, and so on. It was a profound and interesting concept to think about. Without the doctor's shared observation, I would never have made that connection nor observed that reverse progression in Doug's life cycle.

With this heads-up from Doug's doctor, I had time to internalize this possible reality and attempt to emotionally prepare myself. I determined I would view this not as a regression from adulthood back to childhood but would instead choose to understand and accept that Doug was moving forward in his life cycle. Translated, that would mean, for example, that I saw Doug not as a toddler who was not yet potty-trained. Instead, I would choose to see him as an incontinent adult.

I was also committed to continuing to see Doug and relate to him as my husband, as our daughters' dad, and as a peer in his other adult relationships. I desperately wanted and strongly encouraged others to view him and relate to him in the same manner.

The setting where this view was the most difficult to maintain was adult daycare. After he stayed home alone during his early-stage years and then attended a senior center part-time for socialization, I found it necessary to transition him to a full-time adult daycare. It was an incredibly difficult decision, but it was important for his continued safety and ensuring daily life-skill functioning. After a prolonged search and extensive networking, I settled on a program housed in a church complex close to our home. The personnel were kind, the food was good, the cost was affordable, and he was safe. Doug adjusted and, nobly, never complained. He was brave throughout. I was the one who suffered and struggled. It was an extremely painful part of the diminishment in Doug's life cycle. It had been natural to take our daughters to their daycare while we worked. Now it was hard to accept that my husband needed to be in a daycare while I worked. My only mental framework for daycare was our daughters' preschool experience. I cried all the way to work the first day I left each of our daughters at daycare. I did the same the first day I left our daughters' father at his daycare.

My intention to consistently see Doug as an adult with dementia and not as a child was challenged by the reality I saw in his participation in adult daycare. One regular activity he did at his daycare was coloring little ducks or other childish pictures torn from children's coloring books. To no avail, I searched for adult coloring books that had simple lines and shapes to color within but also had pictures that were not childlike with which he could identify. I was more successful in resolving my conflict with the similar flashcard content. I was grateful the personnel were working one-on-one with Doug's long-term memory retention by identifying familiar objects. Like the coloring sheets, the flashcards were pictures of toys and other childhood images. In keeping with my goal to honor Doug as an adult, I made a revised set of flashcards. I took photos of friends and family, as well as many items in our home, such as his computer and musical instruments. I replaced the previously used cards with these, and the daycare folks graciously used them as they worked with Doug.

Every holiday, Doug would bring home from his adult daycare a homemade ornament for our Christmas tree, his handprint, or a trinket box made of Popsicle sticks. Each was eerily similar to the gifts our young daughters brought home from their daycare or preschool. I was able to smile and act excited and express my gratitude to Doug, but inside, I was cringing and resisting.

At the same time at home, Doug attached himself to a stuffed animal dog that had belonged to our older daughter. This was also very hard for me to witness; perhaps I associate stuffies only with small children. To cope, I convinced myself to think of it not as a stuffed animal but as a service dog. Doug would have loved to have had a live service dog, and this stuffed one was serving a purpose for Doug's emotional needs.

Based on my close observations of the beginning life cycles of our children and grandchildren, and the end of Doug's life cycle, the doctor's prognosis did prove to be more fact than fiction. Doug did seem to lose his motor skills and milestones in the opposite developmental order.

It was an honor for me to be married to Doug for thirty-four years, approximately the last half of his life cycle. I view all of our years together as one whole, not split screens of the first half before his diagnosis and the second half living with dementia. It was vital to me to honor Doug's full life cycle. Thus, I committed to accepting his diminishment as part of this cycle while simultaneously committing to enriching the quality of his entire life cycle.

DONNA BROWN BENTON

DONNA BROWN BENTON

Hold Hands and Stick Together

AS AN EDUCATOR and parent, one of my favorite essays is Robert Fulghum's "All I Really Need to Know, I Learned in Kindergarten." In it, he shares his wisdom about how to live, what to do, and how to be. It's chock-full of practical, poetic practices to enrich one's life. A random sample of examples are "take a nap every afternoon" and "remember the little seed in the Styrofoam cup." Fulghum continues until the end, with my personal favorite, "and it's still true, no matter how old you are, when you go out into the world, it is best to hold hands and stick together." When Doug and I navigated the world of Alzheimer's, we embraced Fulghum's wisdom and continued to hold hands to stick together.

From the onset of our relationship, Doug and I held hands. It was the first physical intimacy he initiated. While building our relationship, we would sit for hours talking while holding hands. The physical connection was a symbol of our emotional connection. Hand-holding continued throughout the thirty-five years of our relationship.

From the outside, it could have been perceived by others as simply a habit, but reaching for each other was intentional. How perfectly appropriate that in our marriage ceremony, the priest directed us to join our hands while stating our intentions and exchanging our vows. Two becoming one.

When our daughters were young, they were integrated into our hand-holding. Little hands and big hands entwined, sometimes for warmth, sometimes for safety, and most often for bonding. The arrangement and order of the four sets of hands varied, but the gesture was familiar.

At the time of Doug's death, one of our bridesmaids who was a close friend during the entire duration of our marriage sent me a handmade sympathy card. On the front was a photo she had taken years before when we were enjoying a shared vacation. Unbeknownst to us, she had snapped the picture from behind as Doug and I walked hand in hand, as we were apt to do.

Dear to me Donna,

You held his hand so often as you walked the path of life. You knew the softness, the roughness, the warmth of his touch. You will long for Doug's hand, his embrace, his presence and ache to feel it again.

You will.

This touching sentiment was enclosed in her sympathy card.

In my ongoing grief journey, seeing older couples obviously in love and walking hand in hand arouses in me strong emotions more than almost anything else. How I long to hold Doug's hand again.

Take Me with You!

We are all just walking each other home.

Ram Daas

DONNA BROWN BENTON

Walking Together

EARLY IN OUR dating relationship, the musical *Godspell* was making the rounds at our community theatre venues. Doug and I were often in attendance. The title tells the plotline of the play, a modern translation of the Gospel. Doug and I loved Stephen Schwartz's music and lyrics. Many of these songs from *Godspell* were incorporated into our church community's worship services. "By My Side" spoke to us and stayed with us throughout our love story.

The first verse paralleled our blossoming relationship. We were each hoping for a companion for our life journey. It was a time of warm loving and being loved, a healthy meeting of needs. We were asking of each other:

> Where are you going? Where are you going?
> Can you take me with you?
> For my hand is cold and needs warmth.
> Where are you going?

With the passage of time, our love became permanent; we promised to walk, and sometimes skip, through life together.

> Oh please, take me with you.
> Let me skip the road with you.
> I can dare myself.
> I'll put a pebble in my shoe,
> And watch me walk,
> I can walk and walk.

For thirty-four years, we continued to sing the song and live the song, bravely traveling through life together, hand in hand, side by side, while sometimes painfully experiencing the proverbial pebble in our shoes.

> I shall call the pebble Dare.
> We will talk together about walking
> And when we both have had enough,
> We will take him from our shoes, singing,
> 'Meet your new road.'
> Then I'll take your hand, finally, glad that I am here,
> By your side, by my side.

This song served as an anthem for our sacred, relational pilgrimage. Ram Dass profoundly puts it this way: "We are all just walking each other home." It was an honor walking with Doug as long and as far as we could. When our shared road diverged, I gasped and grasped for the grace to slowly let go of his hand and free him to travel on alone, to return to the home of his soul.

This is a mountain you were born to climb.

DONNA BROWN BENTON

Purposeful Living

IN LATE CHILDHOOD and early adolescence, I had a limited notion of life's purpose. I felt my purpose was to be a teacher. I wanted to give all my future students the positive, life-changing educational experiences my high school teachers afforded me while fulfilling *their* life's purposes. Viktor Frankl, an Austrian psychologist and Holocaust survivor, in his search for life's meaning, suggests that many people, like me, find their purpose in their life's work. I assumed I'd teach my entire career and concluded that was my singular life's purpose.

The passing of time and acquired wisdom awakened in me the realization that my life's purpose is not lifelong. My personal purpose is not fixed but dynamic and ever evolving. Nor is my purpose singular, one and done. I've had many and varied purposes. Being a mother to our daughters and being a grandmother to their children are profound purposes in my life.

In addition to finding meaning through work, Viktor Frankl teaches that we also can find meaning and purpose through love and/or through suffering, the human condition itself. I knew finding meaning while climbing a metaphorical mountain called Alzheimer's would only happen through the love that Doug and I shared. Transforming my vowed love into action would be my motivation, my staying power, to fulfill my purpose of accompanying Doug while ascending the mountain.

Standing at the base, the mountain looked insurmountable, a classic uphill battle. We saw no clear path forward in this uncharted territory. We were afraid of the unknown, as this was our novice climb of this magnitude. The summit wasn't visible, but we still set out and embarked on our Alzheimer's journey.

Sixteen years later, we arrived at the summit. After rest, time, reflection, and renewal, I had a whole new perspective. I had a panoramic view as I looked back from where we came. I was in awe. My fears had been unfounded. The path had been made clear step by step. I had been led by my inner compass and a higher power. I'd been able to fulfill my promise to Doug by accompanying him on this journey. Most profoundly, I fulfilled this life purpose. This was a mountain I was born to climb.

Currently, I am committed to a secondary, related purpose to that of climbing that metaphorical mountain named Alzheimer's. My passion project is to capture, refine, and share our mountain-climbing and summit experience to inspire and reassure others climbing now or in the future.

If you have life, you have purpose. This belief calls me to live openly and with awareness, discovering and discerning my next life purpose.

I earnestly prayed Thomas Merton's prayer originally as a high school student discerning my first vocation to enter a vowed religious community that had a charism of teaching and education.

> My Lord God, I have no idea where I am going. I do not
> see the road ahead of me. I cannot know for certain where
> it will end … And I know that if I will do this, you will lead me
> by the right road although I may know nothing about it.
> Therefore I will trust you always, though I may seem to
> be lost and in the shadow of death. I will not fear, for
> you are ever with me, and you will never leave me to
> face my perils alone.
>
> (Thomas Merton)

Through the years, I preserved this prayer card and continued praying this prayer as I discerned and lived each subsequent purpose. Perhaps this prayer proved most profoundly powerful as I prepared to ascend the mountain of Alzheimer's accompanying my husband. The road was made clear, my fears faded, and I was never left to face my perils alone.

DONNA BROWN BENTON

DONNA BROWN BENTON

Essence Remains

DUE TO MY solid beliefs and certain experiences during our dementia years, I chose not to name Doug's cause of death in his obituary nor in the eulogy at his memorial. I refused to allow his life to be defined solely by his disease. I wanted Doug to be remembered and celebrated for the fullness of his life, his essential nature, his true self.

Before Alzheimer's took its toll on Doug's body, many people commented on how handsome and what a hunk my husband was. I would always agree, as he was tall, dark, and handsome. I would then respond, "Doug is beautiful outside and also inside!" Understandably, when Doug's physical appearance changed, the positive comments about his bodily appearance ceased. But his inner beauty remained. His eyes continued to reflect his depth. I continued to experience his inner beauty through our heart and soul connection. Antoine de Saint-Exupéry, in *The Little Prince*, shares this secret by stating, "It is very simple. It is only with the heart that one can see rightly; what is essential is invisible to the eye."

It pains me to see persons with dementia viewed as lesser than, decreasing in perceived value as the dementia increases. Sadly, this view often affects how the person is respected, treated, and cared for. Dementia patients have inherent dignity, the Divine within. To quote from the carol "Oh Holy Night," "Pining, till He appeared, and the soul felt its worth." Watching Doug's dignity being both respected and disrespected was such an emotional fluctuation for me. With my marriage vows, I had committed to reverence him all the days of my life. I wanted others to revere him as well. In most interactions while living with dementia, people still respected Doug in heartwarming ways. The disrespect sometimes came from pejorative statements made in his presence about his decline, as if he wasn't there hearing and taking it in. To counteract, I would remind Doug that no one determines another's worth and then assure him of his inherent dignity.

A gift that Alzheimer's offers us is the assurance that, despite all the disease takes, the essence remains. No accomplishment could give Doug his essence, and no dementia diminishment could take his essence away from him. His essence was not about functioning or doing. It was about being. I was empowered by learning of the eight words Dana Reeve said to her husband, Christopher Reeve, that saved his life. After his accident that left him paralyzed, Superman was recounting what he could no longer accomplish or do. He ended by saying, "Maybe we should just let me go." Dana responded, "You're still you. And I still love you!" This sentiment could and should be said to each person with Alzheimer's as well.

A common complaint associated with dementia is, "My loved one is no longer themselves. They are gone. That is not my loved one." Their memory may be gone, but the same person is still there. The true self remains. The secret of experiencing the true self of a loved one is not to compare their present to their past or to project into their future. The secret is to simply be with and embrace their present being.

My pilgrimage with Doug from what is external to what is internal was sacred. It involved not disassociating from him but, on the contrary, leaning into the unfolding; I wanted to be present and enjoy Doug's presence. I took comfort in the fact that energy can neither be created nor destroyed but can change forms. While witnessing what was mortal and being destroyed by Doug's dementia, I bore witness to what was untouched by dementia. I learned what is deathless. I always believed, and my experience reinforced, that his soul and spirit are immortal and live beyond time. I believe his essence is perceivable and remains.

DONNA BROWN BENTON

DONNA BROWN BENTON

Compassionate Caring

DOUG WAS HOSPITALIZED again, this time for aspiration pneumonia. His decline was glaring. Alzheimer's had ravaged his body and his brain. Throughout this hospital stay, I held vigil at his bedside. Doug no longer had the cognition to know where he was, nor where I was if I was out of his sight. I chose not to look away or go away. Face-to-face with his condition for days, I was forced to slowly let reality in. This hospital stay felt different. We were long past the predicted average lifespan. We were much closer to the end than the beginning of this journey. Appropriately, the spirit I had maintained was waning; the feelings of grief and imminent loss were growing. My insides felt gutted. Tears streamed easily and unchecked.

The hospital medical team held a discharge-planning meeting with me. They said things like "failure to thrive" and "we've done all we can." They suggested I meet with the hospital's palliative care representative and enroll Doug in Hosparus Health before taking him home. Hosparus Health is the nonprofit provider of hospice services in Kentucky and Southern Indiana. I attended the meeting to appear compliant, but internally, there was zero compliance. I had already decided I would answer, "No, thanks. Not yet." It was all too sudden. I was moving in the right direction but not ready for the quantum leap. I equated *hospice* with the bitter end. I was familiar with all the persuasive hospice advertisements conveying quality of life, not end of life. But they conflicted with my preconceived notions. My intellectual self listened and understood. My emotional self was struggling to catch up. At discharge, I politely declined but promised to leave the door open.

At my next counseling appointment, my counselor helped me open the door a little wider. He listened and received my tearful monologue about my choice dilemma. I shared my fear that somehow my yes to hospice would hasten Doug's death. I still wanted to hold on. I wasn't ready to let him go. We spent the entire counseling session unpacking all my objections and the beliefs from which they flowed. There were two aha moments. I began to see how an affirmative decision could prove to be a win-win for Doug and me. Ultimately, my counselor helped me see that the decision should really be all about Doug. He would benefit greatly from all the wraparound services the Hosparus Health team could offer.

With this additional support in place, I would benefit as well. He reviewed with me how I had struggled throughout with my dual role of being both Doug's wife and his caregiver. This additional team would bring more balance to my life and tip the scales in favor of my role as Doug's wife. Of course, I wanted our marriage to be the priority in our remaining time together. As a result, I was finally able to make the decision I knew all along that I needed to make.

I took my last act of denial and resistance the first day the Hosparus Health team was scheduled to meet and treat Doug. I just couldn't make myself meet the team yet. Being there would make it real. I went to work that day as usual. A close friend, Peggy, who sometimes stayed with Doug and was familiar with Hosparus Health, subbed for me that day. The initiation went well according to both my friend and Doug. Slowly, I opened myself to the team. I had to catch up with Doug, who was already all in.

Our primary nurse on our Hosparus Health team, Joanie Prentice, was an experienced, stellar professional. Personally, she was a gift to both Doug and me. She was kind and caring and relational. As fate would have it, her husband, Sonny, was also a musician who had a chronic disease. Our similarities deepened our connection. The way Joanie connected with Doug was through their mutual love of music. Each visit, she would sing to him, and he would sincerely smile.

Our team's nursing assistant bathed and soothed Doug three days a week. What a gift to both Doug and me. Our social worker was a delight and assisted with sundry services. Our volunteer, Bobby, bonded with Doug, and they quickly became like brothers. Every Sunday afternoon, Bobby would spend quality time with Doug. I could then spend quality time with myself.

It turned out that beginning Hosparus Health was not the immediate end I had feared. The team served us well for close to three years, recertifying Doug every six months. After all this time, our nurse cautioned me that the end was nearing. She knew because when she sang to Doug, he no longer responded with his smile. Due to the fidelity of Hosparus Health, Doug was able to die peacefully in our home.

I never imagined how much support and quality of life the team would bring to us in our home. Doug lived better, maybe even longer. As his wife and caregiver, I felt my load lightened by their ongoing support and services. It freed me to have more time and energy for just being with Doug. That is the very outcome my counselor wisely predicted, helped me envision, and supported me to ultimately choose.

I recently ran across what was described as an archaic definition of *hospice*: "a home lodging providing care or rest to travelers or pilgrims." To me, that definition is neither old-fashioned nor out of date but an accurate description of the care Hosparus Health provided to Doug as a pilgrim, a person journeying to a sacred place.

Volunteer and patient share lyrical bond

Hosparus names 2013 "Year of the Volunteer"

In 1978, a group of people who shared a common bond began meeting. Those early volunteers gave selflessly of their time to bring a new kind of care to our community called "hospice."

From those humble beginnings to Hosparus 35 years later, we still depend on volunteers to help us meet our mission of caring. While our numbers have grown from a few to the 800+, the core of what volunteers do for our patients and families remains constant and their commitment is unwavering. Hosparus volunteers offer a gentle presence and warm friendship to those facing the end of life.

We sat down with Doug Benton, a Hosparus patient; his wife, Donna and his volunteer, Bobby Elder. This is their story:

Bobby Elder says he decided to become a Hosparus volunteer after the organization cared for his mother, Mildred Craig. Bobby's mother spent her final days at the Hosparus Inpatient Care Center. That's where Bobby saw a volunteer in action, spending time with patients who had no family, "I started asking questions about her experience and a few months later, I went through the volunteer training."

He added, "I wanted to give back to the organization that provided so much help to my family."

Now, every Sunday afternoon, Bobby shows up at Doug and Donna Benton's house with his laptop and a malt from Dairy Queen. Although Doug is no longer able to speak, the former musician's face lights up when Bobby enters the room. Bobby and Doug listen to music. Bobby even sings softly to Doug, "I'm not much of a singer but Doug seems to enjoy it," he adds.

"When I think of volunteering, the word that comes to mind is 'friend.' Doug is my friend. On my 50th birthday, I was with Doug; there's nowhere else I wanted to be that day."

Bobby and Doug

Bobby encourages others to consider volunteering for Hosparus and says his initial fear has all but disappeared. "At first, I was afraid I couldn't do it. My advice to new volunteers is 'don't doubt yourself,' you can do it. I think we're placed with people we're supposed to be with. Doug and I have a connection through music."

Bobby says he appreciates the affirmation he gets from Doug's wife, Donna. "She is very appreciative and that gives me a good feeling. Although I know I get far more out of my volunteer experience than anyone can imagine."

Donna fondly calls Bobby a miracle, "The first couple of times Bobby visited; he and Doug listened to music Doug had previously recorded. Then Bobby started bringing his computer and speakers. It's almost like a little concert."

"Thanks to Bobby, I can get out of the house for a bit on Sunday afternoons for some respite. In many ways, before Hosparus came in, it was a solitary journey. To have someone like Bobby care about Doug and show him such respect – I just love that," says Donna.

Thanks to Bobby, Donna has a bit of time to take care of herself. "Bobby's visits are a gift to us both. He's become like a friend and a family member."

Donna concludes, "Hosparus volunteers offer an invaluable gift to families who are caring for loved ones '24/7.' I know I can really count on Bobby to come."

Learn more about volunteer opportunities in your community:

Hosparus Barren River (Bowling Green and surrounding area)
Contact Deborah Faircloth at *dfaircloth@hosparus.org* or (270) 782-7258 x3812.

Hosparus Central Kentucky
(Elizabethtown and surrounding area)
Contact Annette Jones at
ajones@hosparus.org or
(270) 737-6300.

Hosparus Louisville
Contact Laura Harbolt at
lharbolt@hosparus.org or
(502) 719-8920.

Hosparus Southern Indiana
Contact Vonya Gresham at
vgresham@hosparus.org or
(812) 945-4596.

HOSPARUS
Year of the Volunteer
35th Anniversary

DONNA BROWN BENTON

Transforming

SINCE MOVING INTO our house, our family always enjoyed our back porch, which spans the entire width of our home. It brought the outside inside. It provided a connection to the natural world. We socialized and often ate family meals alfresco. After Doug's diagnosis, it became his habitat, his preferred and usual surroundings for the duration. It began as his introverted hideaway, a quiet and peaceful place for his favorite pastime, reading.

Doug always was content outside and enjoyed cutting the grass and feeding the finches and redbirds and our daughters' ever-populating bunnies. Since he was spending so much time on the porch and outdoors alone, I was encouraged to surround our yard with a fence to prevent Doug from wandering away. Sadly, such wandering is a common behavior associated with Alzheimer's. Our next-door neighbor/contractor designed and built our fence of cedar boards taller than Doug. We painted it robin's egg blue. The fence enabled Doug to move in the freedom of his confined space. For me, it was an adjustment to move from viewing the fence only as a barrier to allowing it to become a backdrop. It eventually framed, for me, the theater that nature provided us with right in our own backyard. Our back porch eventually functioned as our grand tier box that was handicap-accessible for Doug's wheelchair.

Doug was on the porch sometimes from sunup to sundown. I'd look forward to joining him after work and on weekends. We both love music, and we enjoyed the music nature provided: the chirping birds, the fountain flowing into the pond water, our wind chimes ringing, and the sound of rain on the roof.

We dined in the open air for many meals. The food nourished our bodies while the environment nourished our spirits. We witnessed the seeming magic of buds turning overnight to blossoms on our dogwood, wisteria, and plentiful perennials.

In Joni Mitchell's "The Circle Game," she sings, "And, the seasons, they go 'round and 'round." Each season provided its own beauty and message about life and death. While we were observing nature, we were also being influenced by it. It was speaking to us and teaching us applicable life lessons. As without, so within. In the midst of our murky times, we were encouraged by the lotus flower's ability to thrive in such a challenging environment in our pond. We watched in awe as this flower emerged from its muddy home to symbolize, for us, strength and resilience. We weathered storms, external and internal, huddled on our porch. Occasionally, our storms were followed by a ray of hope found in a single and even a double rainbow that followed.

The sunlight always brightened our outlook and lifted our spirits in dark times. We never experienced a night that wasn't followed by a day, nor a sunset without a sunrise.

After observing sixteen years of seasons on our back porch, it was the life cycle of the butterfly that held the greatest gift and summed up our own life cycle for us. Ironically, a three-foot metal, multicolored butterfly hung on the porch above our heads the entire time. At an art fair, long before Doug became ill, I purchased this butterfly to serve as a symbol of resurrection and new life for us, not realizing the role it would play in our future.

It was becoming impossible to deny that Doug was in the last season of his life. The change and loss were painful to witness, as I was solely focusing on his death.

But a transformational event was happening within Doug. Synchronicity would have the same transformational event happening before us and for us within view in our backyard. We were witnessing the life cycle of the butterfly. I leaned into the similarities between what we were experiencing in the butterfly and within Doug. Both the butterfly and Doug were inside a cocoon undergoing a metamorphosis. During this process, body tissues were breaking down and reforming as wings. Finally, the butterfly emerged with its soft wings folded around its body. Both journeys reached their crescendo. The butterfly fluttered away, and I pondered my takeaway. Doug's life was not ended but merely transformed.

> We delight in the beauty of the butterfly, but rarely admit the changes it has gone through to achieve that beauty.
>
> (Maya Angelou)

DONNA BROWN BENTON

DONNA BROWN BENTON

Our Memory Garden

DOUG SPENT MORE than two decades of our married life working to renovate our house into our family home. He and I collaborated on every room and project. He was often overheard saying, "Donna is the inspiration, and I am the perspiration." That description of our division of labor was accurate. We each had very different gifts. I envisioned and initiated each home improvement project, sourced and shopped for the supplies, and did the decorating upon completion. Doug supplied all the sweat equity, the heavy lifting, and the manual labor of drywalling, hauling away tons of deconstruction materials, and building closets, to mention just a few of his contributions.

We had completed the renovation of every square inch of the inside and the outside of our property. The only exception was a six-foot-wide strip of land that spanned the entire thirty-six-foot length along the side of our house. We hardly ever visited that outdoor space. Only a utility company employee ventured into this deserted space to read the meter once a month. It was desolate for the first thirty years in our dwelling. Any intended use of this space had been hidden from view the entire time.

I believe that everything comes in the proper time, space, and sequence. Shortly before Doug's impending death, an inspiration for the use of this space came to me. I decided it was meant to be transformed into a memorial garden for Doug. After all the time, energy, and work Doug had poured into his home, this space could become a place of rest for him. I immediately began the implementation of my idea.

Original bricks from our house, harvested from renovations and dismantled chimneys, had been stacked in this space for years. I collaborated with an elderly, experienced landscape mason to plan and design the space. He repurposed the bricks into a path, a bricked-off space to host the garden, with a brick circle of life marking the entrance.

A Louisville sculptor, Albert Nelson, designed and crafted a personal limestone sculpture to symbolize Doug's life and legacy. The sculpture's heart shapes reflect his lifelong love, and its tuning pegs symbolize his lifelong music making. The sculptor involved our daughters and me in the writing and carving of the inscription.

As an outpouring of sympathy and support, my green-thumbed sister-in-law and brother offered to come from Indianapolis to help plant the memory garden the first spring after Doug's death. Intended to be only a one-time gift, they have returned every year for our spring planting ritual.

The desolate land and weeds are gone. The rich soil now supports lush perennial plants, like clematis and ferns. The annuals add color and bursting blooms and blossoms. Window boxes are overflowing with vines and flowering purple heart plants, a salute to Doug and all veterans. Recessed potted plants enliven the brick path.

Because burgundy was our wedding/marriage color, I chose it as the primary color scheme. Cranberry is reflected in the stone embedded in the sculpture, and the same color scheme continues in the trellises, ceramic pots, coral bells, and calla lilies. Lights illuminate the night-blooming moonflowers. A fellow teacher initially gave me the seeds from her moonflowers, and they yearly continue to climb the trellis and grace the garden. A friend built a bench that folds down from the surrounding fence. It's a quiet place where I go to remember Doug and be present with him.

We consecrated Doug's garden on the first anniversary of his death. Yearly on that date, our family gathers there to pray, honor Doug with music, light candles, and experience his presence among us. When we gather, I sense we are standing on holy ground. It has proved to be the perfect and peaceful resting place for Doug.

Daily, I drop in for short stays or to just pass through. Each time I open the gated door to enter, I'm startled again by the beauty and transformation that greet me. I hear myself let out a small gasp of surprise, a sigh, or a breath in response to the spirit in the space. It is peaceful. Rest in peace, dear Doug. Your memory is a blessing.

DONNA BROWN BENTON

DONNA BROWN BENTON

Loss, Change, and Transformation

I WAS PROFOUNDLY INFLUENCED by Anthony Padavano while studying theology in college. His wisdom, shared here, was our saving grace while living with dementia.

> There is a great deal of difference between loss, change, and transformation. A loss is a step backward; a change is an opportunity; transformation is a step forward. The common denominator of these three realities is the fact that one must give up something. It is possible for both loss and change to lead to transformation, but it is not possible for transformation to occur unless something is lost and something is changed.
>
> (Anthony Padavano)

The beginning of Doug's and my Alzheimer's story was only about loss and change. It was natural that we believed that loss and change were all we would experience. We got trapped in the darkness and despair. We assumed we'd live there, never getting past the loss and change. Anthony Padavano offered us a chance to write a different story. He shared the hopeful news that it is possible for both loss and change to lead to transformation, a metamorphosis.

Loss and change were still real, but underneath our surface storyline, we were infusing inspiration, creativity, and spirituality. Slowly, our story was transforming. Loss and change didn't get the last word, the final say. Our story was being transformed into a story of light amidst the darkness.

We, in turn, bring this testimony to you. It is not possible for transformation to occur unless something is lost and something is changed. Your loss and change will be unique, but the possibility of transformation is universal. In this book, I share the small, transformative actions we lived each day, through each stage. I offer our own lived experience as an application of the abstract becoming concrete. May it enable you to live in the midst of, and move through, loss and change to ultimately transform your dementia journey.

DONNA BROWN BENTON

Making Meaning, Moving Forward

THROUGHOUT OUR EXPERIENCE of living with dementia, I attempted to be purposeful and make it as positive as possible for Doug and, in turn, for myself. Throughout the journey and in the years since, I continued to reflect. At the end of our sixteen years, I was grateful to describe myself as having PTSW (post-traumatic stress wisdom) instead of PTSD (post-traumatic stress disorder). Trauma and stress were prevalent, but I was also wiser and not disordered.

What becomes of the wisdom? This question lingered. David Kessler writes about the sixth stage of grief and finding meaning. That certainly resonated with me. I've always coped by trying to make meaning of difficult experiences and growing through them. What a beautifully woven connection—I would find meaning in Doug's Alzheimer's. I would not have had him live with Alzheimer's, nor die from it, in vain. I could give voice to Doug's lived experience. I could turn our pain into passion. I am passionate about sharing my wisdom to inspire others who are coming behind us and are living their dementia experience.

The number of people being diagnosed with dementia will continue to rise while we wait for the cures. Because of the increasing population of older people, that number will increase by millions each future year for decades. I couldn't comprehend the magnitude, and I was sobered by the fact that moving forward, each and every one of us can expect to be affected by dementia.

My focus audience for sharing our meaningful story is at two levels: micro and macro. On a smaller scale, I'd like to influence those who currently are, or in the future will be, companioning persons living with dementia. The sharing of our story has the potential to support and illuminate their lived Alzheimer's experience. My macro vision is that all of these individuals, in turn, could collectively influence the conversation and consciousness about how we view, talk about, and respond to Alzheimer's and other forms of dementia.

During the years of our lived experience and the years since Doug's and my dementia journey ended, I've been laboring to birth this book. Support and encouragement to continue came to me through endless sources of inspiration and persons who shared my purpose and passion. Luckily, I also found a children's book called *What Do You Do with an Idea?* by Kobi Yamada. The inside cover states that it's for "anyone who ever had an idea that seemed a little too big, too odd, too difficult. It's a story to inspire you to welcome that idea, to give it space to grow, and see what happens next." For continued motivation, I read this brief book regularly. The last page summarizes and promises, "Realize what you could do with an idea … You could change this world."

Margaret Mead agrees, "Never doubt that a small group of committed individuals can change the world." Specifically, in this case, we can influence and effect change in the world of Alzheimer's.

Blessing of Memory

You were born
remembering this blessing.

It has never
not been with you,
weaving itself daily
through the threads of
each story, each dream,
each word you spoke
or received,
everything you hoped,
each person you loved,
all that you lost
with astonishing sorrow,
all that you welcomed
with unimagined joy.

I tell you,
you bear this blessing
in your bones.

But if the day should come
when you can no longer
bring this blessing
to mind,
we will hold it
for you.
We will remember it
for you.

DONNA BROWN BENTON

And when
the time comes,
we will breathe
this blessing to you
at the last,
as you are gathered
into the place
where all that
has been lost
finds its way back
to you,
where all memory
returns to you,
where you know yourself
unforgotten
and entirely welcomed
home.

"Blessing of Memory" was shared by Jan Richardson for each of this book's readers. It is a singular blessing from her book *The Cure for Sorrow: A Book of Blessings for Times of Grief.* Jan authored this collection of blessings after her beloved husband's untimely death.

Providentially, a priest friend of mine gifted me with a copy of this book after the death of my beloved husband. Each of the blessings contained in Jan's book blessed me abundantly in my own time of grief. "Blessings of Memory" took my breath away due to my husband's affected memory. In addition to its impact on me personally, I realized this blessing's potential to empower all givers of care and, in turn, our loved ones living with dementia. This realization prompted me to humbly contact the author to request permission to reprint her blessing in my book. She graciously and generously responded affirmatively.

I envision this "Blessing of Memory" becoming the anthem for approaching Alzheimer's. This blessing invites us to hold it and remember it for our loved ones when they can no longer, "And when the time comes, we will breathe this blessing to you …."

The time *has* come for each of us to internalize, live, and bestow this blessing of memory on persons with dementia in our care or within our reach of influence. To each person living with dementia, we pray with words from Jan Richardson's blessing, may you "know yourself unforgotten and entirely welcomed home."

DONNA BROWN BENTON

You have received the neuropathology regarding your spouse. The report shows that he had two different diseases causing his memory, cognitive, and behavioral problems.

The first is Alzheimer's disease that is generally responsible for difficulty with short-term memory and general dementia and the second would be frontotemporal dementia which causes a variety of problems, but specifically abnormal behaviors and poor decision making. The results of this autopsy certainly will be helpful to us in our research to find ways to better treat and diagnose these devastating illnesses.

DONNA BROWN BENTON

Research: Clinical Care and Clinical Trials

SHORTLY AFTER DOUG'S diagnosis of early-onset Alzheimer's, we fortuitously learned of the outstanding reputation of Indiana University School of Medicine and their Indiana Alzheimer's Disease Center (IADC)-Clinical Core. We were desperate for relevant medical knowledge and potential treatments; thus, we were more than willing to drive to Indianapolis regularly to avail ourselves of their comprehensive services. We eagerly scheduled the first available appointment and were accepted to enroll. The benefits proved to exponentially outweigh what was asked of us. This association, which lasted more than a decade, positively shaped the arc of our journey with dementia and continues to yield blessings.

Each visit consisted of a Mini-Mental status test and other diagnostics to track disease progression. We would also be interviewed by clinicians inquiring about Doug's status, any issues that needed attention, and any questions we wanted answered. The doctor would examine Doug, adjust prescribed medicines as needed, and discuss with us his current findings and recommendations. The doctor also served as a conduit for communication with Doug's doctor and medical team at the VA Medical Center in Louisville. Thus, he would follow up after each visit for seamless, coordinated care.

Another advantage of being a patient at IADC-Clinical Core was that Doug was invited to volunteer to be enrolled in clinical trials for which he qualified at various stages of progression of the disease. This research benefited drug development that would determine efficacy for potential dementia treatment. Doug embraced every opportunity for participation. Of course, we both hoped, but would never know, if he was receiving and benefiting from the drug being researched. Even if he received the placebo, and again we wouldn't know, Doug was still honored to participate. These clinical trials offered Doug a chance to help advance research that may lead to treatment or a cure. Doug also left a legacy of medical information through the recording of the progression of his disease.

Our deepest desire was that, by participating in this project, Doug would help further the advancement of research in Alzheimer's and related types of dementia as well as the development of better diagnostic and treatment programs.

Research: Autopsy Results

ALSO, AS A participant in the IADC-Clinical Core Doug was invited, but in no way pressured, to donate his brain upon death to the Department of Pathology Clinical Research and Autopsy. I remember fully how painful it was for Doug to face this reality but how readily he made an affirmative decision. Amid sobbing, he verbalized wanting to help others following him to receive a better prognosis than was available to him at the time of his diagnosis.

The post-autopsy report yielded valuable information. The preliminary report determined two types of dementia present. The final neuropathology report revealed that Doug actually had three types of dementia:

1. Alzheimer disease
2. Frontotemporal lobar degeneration
3. Lewy body disease, limbic

Such a definitive report is only available through autopsy pathology; these findings are not definitively available by a clinician's observation in diagnosis and treatment. The presence of frontotemporal lobar degeneration confirmed what the doctor predicted when Doug lost his ability to speak. Without an autopsy, we would never have known that Doug had three types of dementia. My empathy abounded remembering how long and hard he worked to slow the progression of his condition, not knowing at the time that three forms of dementia were active in his brain.

The other benefit from the pathology research was that Doug's brain showed no evidence of the usual genetic markers. While not a guarantee, this was a tremendous discovery that continues to assure our daughters and lessens our anxiety about the trajectory of their lives. Doug's contribution to this research benefited our family personally as well as furthering research progress.

Research: Progress

O N DOUG'S MEMORIAL sculpture, I had inscribed, in part, "Doug your light shines on …." I didn't know at the time if or how that would happen, only that I hoped it would, and it did. Try to imagine my amazement and excitement when I learned from Bernardino Ghetti, MD, that Doug's brain was part of the research that yielded these breakthrough findings reported in *Nature*, published online on July 5, 2017. The headline read:

IU researchers help provide first look at atomic structures of protein tangles found in Alzheimer's disease INDIANA UNIVERSITY SCHOOL OF MEDICINE

The press release continues, "New research at Indiana School of Medicine gives the most detailed view yet of tau protein structures found in Alzheimer's Disease." A team of scientists, along with Indiana University Distinguished Professor Bernardino Ghetti, MD are the first to present high-resolution structures of tau filament from the brain of a patient with a confirmed diagnosis of Alzheimer's disease. Dr. Ghetti said their findings represent one of the major discoveries of the past twenty-five years in the field of Alzheimer's disease research. "This is a tremendous step forward," Dr. Ghetti said. "It's clear that tau is extremely important to the progression of Alzheimer's disease and certain forms of dementia. In terms of designing therapeutic agents, the possibilities are now enormous." Dr. Ghetti said the new images and analysis could help scientists better understand the molecular mechanisms that cause Alzheimer's disease and identify new strategies for the prevention, diagnosis and treatment of this and other neurodegenerative diseases.

Additionally, there is a great interest and urgency to find the cause and cure for early-onset Alzheimer's. Since Doug was diagnosed at age fifty, his brain is being used as well for their ongoing research and study.

I'm eternally gratified that Doug has contributed in such a significant way to research and its findings. Doug, your light indeed shines on.

> We have to trust that our short little lives can bear fruit far beyond the boundaries of our chronologies. More than ever, I am convinced that death can, indeed, be chosen as our final gift of life.
>
> (Henri Nouwen)

I pray in earnest for Dr. Ghetti and his renowned research. My prayer is for his continued longevity and the bountiful support of the financial endowment to complete the work of his lifelong commitment. We all anxiously await the cures for dementia.

DONNA BROWN BENTON

ACKNOWLEDGMENTS

We all possess different gifts. I will be forever grateful to my family, friends, and colleagues who collaborated with me and contributed their time, talents, and support to make the publication of this book possible. Together, we are whole. I am grateful to the Spirit for gifts given and gifts shared.

Fortuitously, I regularly participated in the Memoir Writing Lab offered at the Trager Family Jewish Community Center in Louisville. Each week, I would share the story I had written, and the other attendees listened and offered support. Our faithful facilitator, a true educator, Jeffery Levy, provided invaluable critiques and coaching.

Angela Lincoln companioned her mother as her caregiver during the same timeframe that I was accompanying my husband. For years, she and I have continued to reflect on our lived Alzheimer's experiences and our resulting values and vision. Our sharing facilitated the birthing of this book.

Bret Walker provided his technology genius, and Janet Lanham was my wonderful word processor. Kelly Haile and Chris Burba contributed in each of these two areas as well.

Editing expertise was provided by Linda Hamilton-Korey, Sheree Koppel, and Erika O'Daniel.

Carole Pfeffer added her literary excellence, and Patrice Trauth added her artistic inspiration.

A picture is worth a thousand words. Gifted photographers Cory Cornelius and Adam Vivona photographed the pictures and visually elevated the included images.

Paula Spugnardi shared her public speaking and communication expertise to assist me with turning my written words into the spoken word.

I'd also like to express my gratitude to author Liz Curtis Higgs for the guidance she offered me through her Called to Write workshop.

Printed in the United States
by Baker & Taylor Publisher Services